"Uncle Curro"

J.R.R. Tolkien's Spanish Connection

José Manuel Ferrández Bru

A biographical approach to Father Francis Morgan Osborne.

His vital and intellectual influence on J.R.R. Tolkien, through his biography, his historical context and his family antecedents.

Francisco Javier (Curro) Morgan Osborne.
Port St Mary (Spain) 1857 - Birmingham (England) 1935

Text Copyright © 2018 José Manuel Ferrández Bru
Cover Design © 2018 Fernando López Ayelo
First published by Luna Press Publishing, Edinburgh, 2018

"Uncle Curro". J.R.R. Tolkien's Spanish Connection ©2018. All rights reserved. No part of this publication may be reproduced, stored in a retrieval system, or transmitted in any form or by any means, electronic, mechanical, photocopy, recording or otherwise, without prior written permission of the copyright owners. Nor can it be circulated in any form of binding or cover other than that in which it is published and without similar condition including this condition being imposed on a subsequent purchaser.

The Osborne Bull is a registered trademark. Permission for its reproduction granted by the Grupo Osborne, S.A.

www.lunapresspublishing.com

ISBN-13: 978-1-911143-35-2

For Leonor & Leonor

Yet I hear you say that bonds such as these do not daunt you. Go your way therefore! Bring to me in your hand a Silmaril from Morgoth's crown; and then, if she will, Lúthien may set her hand in yours.

J.R.R. Tolkien. *The Silmarillion*

And again I remember after the death of Fr. Francis, my "second father" [...] In 1904 we (H[ilary] & I) had the sudden miraculous experience of Fr. Francis' love and care and humour. He was actually of almost exactly the same age as my real father would have been: both were born in 1857, Francis at the end of January, and my father in the middle of February.

The Letters of J.R.R. Tolkien. Letter 332 to Michael Tolkien, January 1972

Contents

Acknowledgments	v
Preface	ix
Introduction	xii
Background	**1**
Port St Mary	3
Illustrious Ancestors	7
The Böhl de Faber Family	14
From Duff-Gordon to Osborne	19
The Wedding of María Manuela	25
Early Years	**31**
The Morgan-Osborne Family	33
Education in England	42
Vocation	49
The Community of the Oratory	56
Life Between Birmingham and Port St Mary	61
Maturity	**67**
The Tolkiens	69
A New Life	76
A Rainy Day (A Day in the Life)	85
The Love Affair	88
The Great War	94
The Fulfilled Duty	98
Last Years	102
Epilogue	**107**
Intellectual Influence on Tolkien	109
Tolkien and Cardinal Newman	116
Tolkien and the Spanish Civil War	121
Barrels Out of Bond	129
Appendix	133
Bibliography	142

Acknowledgments

My dear reader, you now have in your hands the result of a long journey that began more than a decade ago as a mere amusement but, over time, became something more tangible. However, this story begins even further back, in the 1980s, with a teenager discovering *The Lord of the Rings* and being seduced and moved for life by images and feelings he did not fully understand then. Subsequently, it arrived in conjunction with an increased fondness for the works of J.R.R. Tolkien, encountering other enthusiasts, and a personal evolution that was necessary in order to understand and explain those early sensations.

I couldn't say exactly when I heard of Francis Morgan for the first time, though it surely must have been while I was reading one of Tolkien's biographies. I must confess that, at the time, he passed quite unnoticed by me, perhaps because of the limited attention paid to him by Tolkien's biographers to his role, along with it being from such an early period in the author's life. The fact is that, although I was intrigued by his hardly-mentioned link with Spain, the surname Morgan did not particularly arouse my curiosity.

However, many years later, without actively looking for information on the subject, chance put a datum about him before me, something apparently insignificant but most likely the catalyst for everything: his second surname. This was his maternal surname, which had been forgotten and relegated by the Anglo-Saxon world; a surname so important in establishing kinships: Osborne. Thus, I cannot forget how, in my first contact with the Osborne family (his only living relatives today), Tomás Osborne, whom I owe so much, told me about his "Uncle Curro". That would be the beginning of my inquiries, with the clear goal of rescuing someone who had been forgotten by time.

My profession is little related to historical research and literature but, with passion and instinct, the story of a life, a family, and a time, was rebuilt and gave rise to something coherent. In addition, when, in 2006, I dared to submit an early version of my work to the renowned Premio Algaba de Biografía e Investigaciones Históricas and became a finalist, I knew that the story carried genuine interest.

After I published several articles and essays on the subject, which made it known in specialised areas, finally, in 2013, a first version of the work in book form saw the light. That said, it was limited to the Spanish market and had some small problems, due to the precariousness of the Spanish publishing industry outside of the large publishing houses.

Now, five years later, I am pleased to present this edition, corrected and enlarged, with a greater number of images and graphic resources. Above all, it is aimed at an international level, which, in a way, represents closing the circle.

*

During this long process, many people have assisted me. Above all, I must single out my wife and my daughter, whom I often neglected while I was concentrated on an absorbing task. Without their support and their love none of this would have been possible, and this work is largely their work as well.

Tomás Osborne Gamero Cívico, fifth Count of Osborne and honorary president of the company of the same name, deserves special mention. I stole much of his precious time, embarking him on this trip to try reconstruct the life of one of his relatives. His information, and access to the Osborne Archive, allowed me obtain data that would have been otherwise impossible to find.

The Tolkien family must also be recognised. After informing them of my research, Adam Tolkien, on behalf of his father Christopher (literary executor of J.R.R. Tolkien), was kind enough to respond and encourage me, which he reiterated when I met him in 2008. Along with this, Priscilla Tolkien, the author's daughter, politely shared some of her memories of Morgan with me, revealing unpublished stories of her family that were of the highest value in understanding the importance of Fr. Francis in Tolkien's daily life.

It is also important to highlight the role of the great scholar John Garth, author of *Tolkien and the Great War*, who encouraged me from the beginning phases of my work right through until the present moment, including writing an extraordinary preface for this edition. I also owe him for the clue about Tolkien's homage to Morgan in the gnomic lexicon. Helios de Rosario Martínez helped me with this matter (in fact, he supported me in many others topics).

Ana Becerra Fabra, of the Municipal Archive of El Puerto de Santa María, has been an extraordinary collaborator who researched among the dense archives of her city and revealed some extremely interesting information. I have to thank Javier Maldonado Rosso too, for putting me in touch with her. Bernardo Rodríguez Caparrini, also from El Puerto de Santa María, was a methodical researcher and attentive companion in one of my visits to the city. His information on the Osborne children's school years was very illustrative. Nearby, in Cadiz, Manuel Ravina Martín (now Director of the Archivo General de Indias) and Carlos Rodway Chamorro, from the Archivo Histórico Provincial, provided me with notarial documents, wills, declarations of property, etc. from the Morgan family, which remain in that institution.

On the other hand, the assistance of Fr. Paul Chavasse, former Provost of the Birmingham Oratory, and postulator of the cause of canonisation of Cardinal Newman, informed me of issues that would have been forgotten without his help and, in any case, impossible to find out from Spain. Anthony Tinkel, of The Oratory Schools Association, was also an important supporter for the development of various aspects of this work related to the school where the Morgan brothers attended.

Anders Stenström gave me firsthand information about the coded letter written by Tolkien in 1904, which is preserved in the Bodleian Library.

In Nottingham, I received the support of Brenda M. Pask, librarian at the Parish Church of St. Mary Magdalene in Newark. I should also like to thank Fr. Brian Dazeley of Holy Trinity, also in Newark, who put me in touch with Fr. A. P. Dolan, the archivist of the Catholic Diocese of Nottingham. His counterpart in Birmingham, Fr. John Sharp, archivist of the Catholic Diocese of Birmingham, was also very kind in his answers.

Tom Horwood, a scholar of the English Roman Catholic Church at the time of Cardinal Manning, helped me in my inquiries on the Catholic University of Kensington and put me in contact with Fr. Nicholas Schofield, archivist of the Diocese of Westminster, who, despite the limited success of his research, was particularly cordial.

I must thank Marion Nicholas, and especially Ivonne Solomon, for their help in collecting data on the Galtons, Morgan's English cousins. I am equally indebted to Gillian Grute, who provided me with data on the Shaws. Thanks to David Villanueva, who provided additional information about his family, useful for the chapter "A Rainy Day", where I mention some of his ancestors.

Thanks to the interest of Jane Flower, the librarian at the British Historical Society of Portugal, I was able to obtain much of the information related to the Morgans and their contacts with Portugal.

In London, Nik Pollard from Richmond's Local Studies, and Mike Cherry from Twickenham Local History Society, helped me in my inquiries about the Morgan family's relationship with South London. Similarly, Dave Payne of the Southwark Cathedral gave me information about Aaron Morgan.

From Australia, Robert Hinii shared details with me on a book that once belonged to Fr. Morgan, having miraculously rescued it from a bookstore on a distant continent.

I also have to thank the following for their explicit support and encouragement during the long gestation of this work: Paul Shrimpton, author of the excellent and highly illustrative *A Catholic Eton?: Newman's Oratory School*; Eduardo Segura, reference for the Tolkien Spanish scholars; the poet Enrique García-Maiquez who, thanks to his articles, informed the media about Tolkien's Spanish connection; Adolfo Blanco Osborne, a member of this distinguished family, with whom I shared long conversations full of data and knowledge; the historian Luis Arias González.

I'd also like to acknowledge my colleagues from the Tolkien Society of Spain, who read this book before it was published and sent me their comments: Paco Soliva, Paco Sempere, Antonino Vázquez, and Fernando Frías Sánchez, who suggested the idea concerning the peculiarities of Arcos de la Frontera. It is also worth noting at this point the work of Jorge López Prieto, whose indications and corrections have been extremely useful; equally, all those who have helped me spread my work, such as María Jesús Lanzuela, Mónica Sanz, Joan Carles Jové, and Santiago Álvarez, amongst many others. In any case, my gratitude extends to all members of the Tolkien Society of Spain, whose mere existence is a constant stimulus.

This list would not be complete without remembering the sadly deceased Maggie Burns and Daniel Grotta. Maggie Burns, of the Birmingham Local Studies and History, and a member of the Tolkien Society, helped me find extremely valuable data on Tolkien's and Morgan's relationships with Birmingham. Daniel Grotta, author of a biography on Tolkien, was very kind in his answers on certain matters related to the contacts he had established at the Birmingham Oratory, while he was researching for his book in the seventies. Among these contacts, for instance, were some companions of Morgan.

Finally, it is essential to point out some necessary collaborators in this work. Fernando Lopez: friend, incomparable artist and erudite who, besides making an incredible cover, was the discoverer of the peculiarities of El Tajo del Águila. I also evidently have infinite gratitude for the whole team at Luna Press Publishing, among them my editor Robert S Malan, but especially my publisher, Francesca Barbini, counselor, friend, and a great professional, who shaped this work.

Preface

When Father Francis Morgan stepped in to the young JRR Tolkien's life, it was to fill not one breach but two – the death of his mother Mabel when he was just twelve, but also the death of his father Arthur eight years earlier. Tolkien later referred to Fr Francis as his 'second father' and remained inexpressibly grateful for his warmth, humanity and understanding.

José Manuel Ferrández Bru's richly informative biography of Fr Francis likewise fills a breach. This one goes all the way back to 1977 and the publication of Humphrey Carpenter's authorised biography of Tolkien – a book which sketches beautifully, but skimps on detail and texture, leaving the curious reader always wanting to know more.

There is indeed much more to learn about this young man who went on to become a lifelong resident of the Birmingham Oratory. And so much of it makes the reader pause to think of Tolkien.

I will mention just one instance. In a performance at the Oratory School, the young Francis played elderly nurse – according to one eyewitness conjuring up 'the apparition of a veritable hag ... with such spirit and humour as I never remembered before'. Tolkien himself had a strikingly similar moment of stage glory, playing Mrs Malaprop in Sheridan's *The Rivals* when he was 19 – 'a real creation, excellent in every way and not least so in make-up', according to his school newspaper.

I suspect there is a connection here; that Tolkien took some of this high-spirited enthusiasm for performance from his guardian. The importance of this should not be underestimated. One of the engines that drove Tolkien's creativity was the pleasure of performing. This is the man whose talent at writing first bloomed as a way of showing off in school and college meetings and magazines, who would open lectures on *Beowulf* by striding on stage declaiming the poem like an Anglo-Saxon *scop*, and whose *Hobbit* and *The Lord of the Rings* were read aloud long before they ever reached print.

This new book paints a portrait not only of Francis Morgan but of the dynasty and the sherry trade of Cádiz – a small world unto itself – from which he emerged into independent life. It will satisfy the most hobbit-like hunger for family history.

Perhaps no other reader will get quite as big a surprise reading this new book as I did. It was an entirely personal one. When I saw that the teenage

Francis Morgan had lived near Regent's Park in London at 138 Harley Street, I did a double take. That address is right next door to the house in which I began writing *Tolkien and the Great War.* Trivial coincidence, but it suddenly made me recognise *JRR Tolkien's Spanish Connection* for what it is: a doorway back to a time where familiar things suddenly take on unfamiliar perspectives.

Time travel was much on Tolkien's mind in 1937 when he began a story called *The Lost Road*. It was written two years after Fr Francis's death, when the Spanish Civil War raged as a terrible example of what might lie around the corner for Europe and the world. When the modern-day philologist Alboin travels back in time to the doomed land of Númenor, the troubles he finds there look startlingly contemporary.

But Alboin doesn't land bodily in Númenor, like HG Wells's archetypal time traveller among the Eloi and Morlocks; instead, he sees everything through the eyes and with the consciousness of a Númenórean. It has been suggested that Alboin's father Oswin owes something to Fr Francis, especially in his quiet, paternal anxiety as the teenage Alboin's obsession with 'Eressëan' language threatens to derail his chances of getting into Oxford University.[1] If so, Tolkien's portrait of Francis Morgan is the most touching piece of time travel in the whole story – an attempt to revisit his own youth, but to see it through the eyes of the 'second father' he missed so much.

My own research has turned up one additional fact of significance for the biographies of these two men. When he died, Fr Francis Morgan left Tolkien and his brother Hilary £1,000 each.[2] It was an enormous sum in those days. For Tolkien it may have helped lighten the burden of family finances that weighed him down and forced him to fill so much of his 'free' time by marking exams for extra money. It may perhaps have released some time for the renewed work on his legendarium which seems to have been a feature of the following two years, which saw the publication of *The Hobbit* and the commencement of its sequel.

But Tolkien knew his debt to his guardian ran much deeper than anything money could buy. He recalled that after his mother's death he had 'the sudden miraculous experience of Fr Francis' love and care and humour'.[3] The phrasing echoes Tolkien's landmark paper *On Fairy-Stories*, where he defines the supreme fairy-tale moment, 'the sudden joyous "turn"' he calls *eucatastrophe*:

---

1. Diana Pavlac Glyer and Josh B. Long, 'Biography as Source: Niggles and Notions', in Jason Fisher (ed.), *Tolkien and the Study of His Sources*, McFarland, Jefferson, 2011.
2. Archives of the Birmingham Oratory, cited by permission.
3. Humphrey Carpenter, (ed.), *The Letters of J.R.R. Tolkien*, Houghton Mifflin, Boston, 1981, Letter 332.

It is a sudden and miraculous grace: never to be counted on to recur. It does not deny the existence of dyscatastrophe, of sorrow and failure: the possibility of these is necessary to the joy of deliverance; it denies ... universal final defeat and in so far is *evangelium*, giving a fleeting glimpse of Joy, Joy beyond the walls of the world, poignant as grief.

John Garth

Introduction

No one is outside the influence of the people surrounding him, and even the trendsetters, who inspire fashions or become social models are, to a large extent, the result of the ties that they established with other people throughout their life, either voluntarily or because of circumstances.

In the field of literature these influences are rather evident, since certain individuals, through their vital relationship with an author, serve as inspiration for characters and stories that appear in the author's works.

In this book we will look at the life of one of these people: Fr. Francis Xavier Morgan, one of those "minor players" in the biography of John Ronald Reuel Tolkien, the famous 20th century writer and author of original contemporary icons such as *The Lord of the Rings*.

Their relationship dates back to Tolkien's infancy, when his recently widowed mother made the difficult decision, especially in that historical context, of converting to Catholicism along with her children. Morgan, a mature Roman Catholic priest of Spanish origin, was a support for them.

The relationship between the priest and the Tolkien family intensified after the conversion. In fact, the last will of Tolkien's mother (who died a few years later), fearful that after her death her two children would be forced to abandon the practice of Catholicism, was to appoint Morgan as their guardian.

Fr. Francis Morgan became one of the leading guides for Tolkien. After the death of his mother and until his coming of age (and even after), he dealt with his religious training but was also concerned with his studies, his care and his future.

Indeed, he was primarily responsible for ensuring that Tolkien attended Oxford University, thanks to his financial support and, indirectly, giving his initial opposition to Tolkien's relationship with the woman who later would become his wife, Edith Bratt.

Unfortunately, his firm stance against a young love with poor prospects (at that moment) for Tolkien's career and, in general, for his future, gives a distorted view of Morgan, and his alleged unfair severity is far from reality. Moreover, his role in this issue has been the trigger for a covert and unjust animosity towards him, making him one of the people who had a close relationship with Tolkien not considered wholly positively by the author's biographers.

In a way, one of the primary objectives of this study is to present an image closer to reality of Francis Morgan; a complex task because he has usually been described in a distorted manner, given the importance acquired by Tolkien. It is an unpleasant portrait, depicting Morgan as noisy and vulgar, his personality defined as petty and shortsighted, and his temperament invariably presented as firm and intransigent.

However, these views are stereotypes rather than realities and Morgan's influence on Tolkien, a little surprisingly, exceeds what traditionally has been assumed. He was a man who, despite the logical moderation of a member of the Church, had no problems showing his warm and open temperament in a society like the British one, which was largely characterised by control and composure. It is very likely that his apparent lack of intellect and erudition is but a reflection of an extroverted personality, that was striking in the social environment where he lived.

What is not in doubt, and is something barely highlighted by Tolkien's biographers and scholars, is the intense relationship that they shared throughout their lives, almost as if they were biological father and son. The contact between them during the author's early years is frequently mentioned, but as soon as Tolkien came of age, Morgan is hardly cited.

However, this does not mean that their bond ceased or was lessened by some kind of animosity that Tolkien might have felt towards him, because of Morgan's early opposition to his romantic relationship with his future wife. On the contrary, in the years in Leeds, when Tolkien became professor, Morgan was a regular visitor of the Tolkien family, as he was too in the early thirties, once they moved to Oxford.

This book will also reveal how Francis Morgan came from a family with a significant history in the world of letters, which certainly gave him an intellectual background that, even indirectly, impacted on Tolkien.

It is often mistakenly assumed that his personal universe was neither sophisticated nor stimulating, yet his life and relationships were quite inspiring and surely Tolkien inherited something of his vital richness. When digging deeper into his biography, we meet with someone whose life was spent between two worlds. On the one hand, in England, where his vocation led him, and where he became Fr. Francis Morgan; on the other, in Andalusia, Port St Mary, his place of birth, a sunny and cheerful home, where he was Curro Morgan, or simply "Uncle Curro, who is a priest in England".

Therefore, to understand him and his influence, it is necessary to rebuild his life story, which means putting together, in a sort of time travel, a jigsaw puzzle whose pieces are scattered between Spain and England.

Background

Port St Mary

The province of Cadiz, in the south of Spain, is known since antiquity by its ability to attract peoples of varied origins. Both in the district of the bay, flanked by the Atlantic Ocean, and in the interior areas, there were successive settlements; the Phoenicians, Greeks, Romans, Arabs and Christians who occupied the lands of Cadiz, transformed them into a crossroads for travellers and merchants.

In particular, concerning Port St Mary, leaving aside the Palaeolithic and Phoenicians vestiges of high archaeological value found near the current city, tradition has it that the town was founded by Menestheo, an Athenian leader. After the Greeks, Port St Mary's was conquered by the Romans. It was later annexed by the Muslims in 711, reconquered by King Alfonso X in 1260 and, from then on, linked to the history of Spain. It was involved directly in several important events, some related to the discovery of the Americas or the trade with the New World, but also with significant episodes of the complex Spanish 19th century.

Nonetheless, we cannot understand Port St Mary outside the context of the Bay of Cadiz, today an important encounter point for the main current nomads: the tourists. The configuration and the attractiveness of the area are reasons enough to explore it and the ubiquitous presence of the ocean, which divides two lands worthy of being visited, is another incentive to do so. On the south side of the bay is Cadiz, the urban and cosmopolitan capital, overflowing with history, as proudly reflected in its monuments and emblematic buildings. Opposite, with the Atlantic in between, are Port St Mary, Rota and, further on, Chipiona and Sanlucar de Barrameda, where the Andalusian great river Guadalquivir flows into the ocean.

In his novel, *The Restlessness of Shanti Andia*, Pío Baroja poetically describes the view of the Bay of Cadiz:

> [...] We would gaze down over Cadiz Bay, usually intense blue. Far off, we could see Rota and Chipiona, their white houses shining in the sun. Then, the low coast forming a series of reddish sandbanks to Port St Mary, and in the ground the mountains of Jerez and Grazalema, turning purple toward nightfall and running in a strange silhouetted line along the horizon.[1]

---

1. Pío Baroja, *The Restlessness of Shanti Andia*, Signet Classic, New York, 1960, p. 113. Pío Baroja (1872-1956) was a Spanish writer, generally associated with the denominated Generation of the 98. He is one of the foremost novelists of the country during the first half of the 20th century.

For millennia, there has been close contact between Port St Mary and Cadiz, connected as they are by a short boat ride. Nowadays, this journey is another tourist attraction. Sailing the few miles between the towns gives a feeling of being transported into the past and imagining the comings and goings of ancient peoples, as you sail past the houses of Port St Mary, through the estuary of the river Guadalete, the little brother of Guadalquivir.

In a sense this river is the *spine* of the western part of the region of Cadiz and, moving upriver, we can get an overview of its towns and territories. The river leads us to Sierra Morena, once a bandits' refuge, but now a unique land with its White Towns, such as Arcos de la Frontera, built on a cliff, or Bornos, a place of peace and serenity.

The presence of so many cultures in the area is evident from their archaeological footprints as well as through the habits and traditions they have left behind. It should be noted, for instance, the variety of wines and liquors obtained from vines brought by the Phoenicians. Specifically, in the area surrounded by the cities of Jerez de la Frontera, Sanlucar de Barrameda and Port St Mary, popularly known as "The Shire", the production of alcoholic beverages became more than a tradition, growing into a productive export business.

According to Greek historians Strabo and Eutymos, the Phoenicians brought vines to the area around the 11th century B.C.E. and, shortly after, they began to ship their wines along the Mediterranean. These primitive liquors were created by boiling the fermented grape-juice to resist long trips, hence the high levels of alcohol. Due to the imperfections of the fermentation process, it was necessary to mix them with water and add spices. The commercialisation of wine and their volume of export increased with the Roman conquest of the region and Rome then became its primary destination.

In the Middle Ages, the vineyards survived the Arab conquest, despite their religious prohibitions on drinking. When the Christians reconquered the land, an emerging wine industry became known and celebrated even beyond the Iberian Peninsula. There is documented evidence showing that local wines were already sent to England in the 12th century, where they began to be known as *sherry* (English name of Jerez [de la Frontera]).

Eventually, sherry acquired enormous popularity among the British, which is still evident in their culture. For example, there are multiple references in Shakespeare's works, such as in Henry IV:

> If I had a thousand sons, the first humane principle I would teach them should be to forswear thin potations and to addict themselves to sack [sherry][2]

---

2. William Shakespeare, *Henry IV*, Simon & Schuster, New York, 2005, Act IV, Scene II, p. 5.

They also launched numerous military and commercial operations aimed at its control. After documented acts of piracy, perpetrated by, among others, Sir Martin Frobisher and Lord Wimbledon, who attacked and sacked the area, their tactic changed to a focus on trade. From the late 17th century, and especially during the 18th and 19th centuries, they established British commercial houses in the region, often founded by adventurers or romantics searching for fortune in Andalusia.

Port St Mary and Jerez de la Frontera, just over five miles apart, along with Cadiz at first, were the places where most of them settled. The surnames of those pioneers who, through skill, hard work and sound business instincts, raised major vintners' companies, have been preserved into present day as known brands. Thus, names such as Garvey, Terry, Osborne or Sandeman remind us of their origins and of this era of flourishing trade.

Specifically, Port St Mary, once a prosperous export centre for the New World, especially due to the relevance acquired from the *Cargadores de Indias* (exporters to the Americas of products of all kinds, whose traces still remain in the city with their House-Palaces), saw its glory revived thanks to the wine trading houses.

These houses, particularly those of British origin, were eventually consolidated, and the fortunes of their founders increased in parallel to their social position. They certainly shaped a new social group, but in a different way to other places, where a similar process took place, for example in Portugal.[3]

Those foreigners and their descendants were Hispanicising and acquiring the habits and traits of their new homeland, such as religion, language, and customs. Although they did not completely give up their British origins, successive generations, often as a result of marriages with Spaniards, gave rise in the 19th century to an influential Spanish-British collective, well connected both in Spain and the United Kingdom.

This group was no stranger to all the events of the 18th and, in particular, the 19th century: the Napoleonic invasion and the War of Independence against his army, the subsequent Spanish dynastic chaos, endless numbers of changes of governments, regencies, pronouncements and more or less successful revolutions, the loss of the Spanish colonies overseas, the first Spanish Republic, and a complicated process of monarchical restoration at

---

3. At Porto and Lisbon, the main places of the British immigration in Portugal related to the trade (in particular that of liquors), the relationship among the native Portuguese and the foreigners happened in a different way. The social mixing which occurred in Spain (intermarriage, castilianisation of names, religious conversion, and so forth) did not take place in Portugal. There, the Britons mainly maintained their religion and habits, establishing their own meeting places, erecting Anglican churches and even their own cemeteries. Although, at Jerez and Port St Mary, there are examples of this attitude, in the 20th century, it was exceptional to find a descendant of Britons more devoted to their roots than to Spain. In Portugal, however, this differentiation was ordinary almost until modern times.

the end of the century.

However, in the internal history of the area, we find other particularly relevant facts, beyond politics, that can help us understand Port St Mary's progress and growing prosperity. Perhaps the most prominent were the changes in the winemaking process. Instead of basing production on young grape juices (fermented at the point of destination) or on liquors aged by the traditional system of vintages, the significant increase in British demand for homogeneous wines with a smooth taste meant that wines began to be produced with a system called *criaderas* and *soleras*. As a result of this radical transformation, larger wineries began to appear, known as *cathedrals of wine*[4] and, at the same time, the industry was strengthened and consolidated as significant levels of exports were ensured.

Thanks to the dynamism and adaptability of the wine trade and its trading links, the Bay of Cadiz (in particular Jerez de la Frontera and Port St Mary) enjoyed a booming economy in the mid-nineteenth century that was the envy of the rest of Spain. It is certainly difficult to accurately quantify the impact of the production of alcoholic beverages on the economy of the area. However, both towns became the most prosperous in the region, and in this period it accounted for over 60% of their income (most of which naturally came from wine industry exports).[5]

In this context of prosperity, with winemakers and traders of British origins rising to the top of their social sphere, and Isabel II Queen of Spain overseeing the transition between the governments of General Espartero and General O'Donnell, a child was born. From one of the most prominent families of Port St Mary, Francis Xavier Morgan-Osborne arrived into the world in January 1857.

---

4. The *criaderas* and *soleras* system, in contrast to the more usual one of *añadas* (vintages), where the harvest of each year ages without mixing with ones from other years, allows for a special ageing process. This process combines, using a systematic method, the wines of different harvests and produces homogeneous liquors, independent of the year of production. There are several variants, such as *Fino, Amontillado, Oloroso, Palo Cortado, Pale cream, Cream, Pedro Ximénez* and *Moscatel*. This system required the construction and installation of a system of cellars, wide and diaphanous (hence the denomination of *cathedrals*), big warehouses, where many barrels were stored and the slow but constant process of production of the liquors was carried out. At Port St Mary, as in Jerez de la Frontera, the cellars are now part of the urban landscape and, with their undeniable monumental character, contribute to the singular architecture of both cities.

5. The period of greatest exports was in the early 70s of the 19th century, reaching around 100,000 boots (the barrels) in 1873 (the highest amount until a hundred years later). About 90% of them were bound for the British market, while the rest was distributed between the Americas and continental Europe. The boots were the means used for distribution of alcoholic beverages. In fact, the sale of bottled products was not commonplace until the 20th century.

Illustrious Ancestors

The surname "Morgan" is one of the most emblematic of Wales. Traditionally, it was agreed that its etymology meant "born of the sea", assuming that it derived from *mor-gen-i* (being *mor*, the Welsh expression for "sea", and *geni*, for "giving life"). However, current and more reliable theories suggest that its origin is *Morcant*, a primitive form of Morgan; *Mor* is linked with the Welsh words *mawr* ("great"), and *cant* ("hundred" or, in an alternative meaning, "crowd"); therefore, "great crowd".

Well-known people with Morgan as their surname are found ever since the Middle Ages. According to family tradition, Morgan's ancestry can be traced to Cadifor Fawr and his son Bledri, who were Welsh leaders at the time of the Norman conquest. Thanks to their good relationship with the Normans, they were granted lands in the region of Monmouthshire, in South Wales. Among the many branches of the family, arguably the most important are the Morgans of Tredegar, whose family tree stretches back to the 14th century. It gives us a picture full of distinguished Welsh historical people, who played typical roles in the finest social elite, as sheriffs, members of parliament, and so forth.[1]

The Tredegar were ennobled, first with a barony and, later, with a lineage of viscounts. This privilege was enjoyed by some of its most famous members, like Sir Charles Gould-Morgan (who occupied the principal political and military position of Judge Advocate General), Godfrey Charles Morgan, the first Viscount Tredegar, and participant in the legendary Charge of the Light Brigade during the Crimean War and, in the 20th century, Evan Morgan, fourth Baron and the second Viscount Tredegar, who was famous for his eccentricities and odd friends.

The family of Fr. Francis Morgan always boasted about their relationship with the Morgans of Tredegar. It seems that they emerged from a branch that had separated from the main Tredegar trunk around the 17th and 18th

---

[1]. Legend links the famous buccaneer Henry Morgan with the Tredegar family. Over the centuries, it was argued that he was a member of the household and, either because of his personality, or because of being kidnapped as a boy, he began a life of adventure at sea that led him to become one of the best known and successful pirates in history. It seems, however, that the relationship with the Tredegars is less direct than has been assumed. Everything indicates that he was the son of a worker, or a tenant of a family farm. The story of his kidnapping as a boy seems plausible, and is a suitable starting point for an amazing biography. His acts of piracy made him the terror of the Spanish and the Dutch in the Caribbean and, during the last years of his life, he was rewarded by the British Empire with honours and important appointments, such as governor of the island of Jamaica.

centuries, who had settled in London. It was from this offshoot that John Morgan, one of the most famous among the Morgans of Tredegar of this era, known as "the Merchant", established himself in London, where he amassed a vast fortune.

The first Morgan related to Fr. Morgan, of whom there is a specific reference, was his great-great-grandfather Thomas Morgan, who lived in the early 18th century. His daughter Elizabeth, apparently his eldest child, was born in London and was baptised at the church of St Sepulchre.

In addition to Elizabeth, Thomas Morgan had three sons. We only know the name of the younger one — apart from his sister, he was the only child who had descendants. He was called Aaron and was born in 1742. Unlike his sister, and probably some of his older brothers, Aaron was not born in London, but in Sea Mills, a suburb of Bristol. There was also Hester Maies, born in 1711, who married Thomas Morgan in 1755, although it is unknown whether she was his first wife.

Despite Roman remains, Sea Mills, separated from Wales by the estuary of the River Severn, was a forgotten place until the early 18th century, when several short-lived maritime initiatives began, such as the construction of a wet dock and the start up of a whale fishery enterprise.

It seems that Thomas Morgan settled in Bristol with the idea of engaging in shipbuilding, and records suggest that he became the owner of a ship. However, other sources indicate that he had other work, as he is described as a *peruke maker* (wigmaker) in several documents. His life, like that of two of his sons, was short-lived (by 1768 he appears as *deceased* in a list of Bristol Freeholders and Freemen that included his daughter and his son-in-law). Elizabeth married a cordwainer of Bristol named Edward Jones, and they had at least five children mentioned in Aaron's will.[2] Regarding the other two sons of Thomas Morgan, the eldest liked life at sea, but he died on his first voyage, during a revolt of the slaves carried by his ship, and the second died of tuberculosis.

Thus, Aaron continued the family line that led to Fr. Francis Morgan. In fact, he became a cornerstone of their history, responsible for their wealth, and promoter of the business which would occupy them for over a century. His decision to settle in London in the late 18th century proved crucial to what came later, especially his work as a clerk in the wine trade company, Dixon & Langston.

Previously, he had been recommended to Sir Thomas Mannock of Giffords Hall, in Suffolk, a Roman Catholic aristocrat with whom he struck

---

[2]. Prerogative Court of Canterbury and related Probate Jurisdictions: Will Registers. Name of Register: Kent Quire Numbers: 452 - 501. Will of Aaron Morgan, Wine Merchant of Savage Gardens , City of London. Held by: The National Archives - Prerogative Court of Canterbury. Date: 29 August 1820, Reference: PROB 11/1633/373. Subjects: Trade and commerce | Wills and probate.

up a cordial friendship. In fact, it seems that if Aaron had agreed to abandon his faith and convert to Catholicism, he would have received a large inheritance from Mannock. Interestingly, Mannock was related through his second wife to the Moulin-Browne family, one of whose descendants, Stanislaus du Moulin-Browne, would be a colleague of Fr. Francis Morgan in the Birmingham Oratory more than a hundred years later.

Focusing again on Dixon & Langston, the firm was dedicated to the trade of wine and spirits, and originated from a company founded in 1715 by a merchant called Haughton of St John's Gate at Clerkenwell, London, who traveled to Porto to start a trade business. Since the mid-eighteenth century, the company had been managed by James Langston (related to Haughton), who was subsequently associated with Charles Dixon and his son of the same name. Although Aaron Morgan joined the firm as a mere clerk, eventually he become one of the owners, and his descendants would run the company in the following decades.

Until 1840, in what could be considered the early period of the company, its headquarter was at 13 Savage Gardens, next to the Tower of London. However, due to changes in partners, its name was modified over time. It was called Langston & Dixon as far as 1800, but from then until 1810 it became Dixon, Brett & Morgan (indicating the inclusion of Aaron Morgan as business associate, together with a man called James Brett). Later, until 1835, it was renamed Dixon, Morgan & Co., and from 1835 to 1840 was known as Morgan & Saunders & Co.

An indirect reference helps us to learn some telling details about the business organisation in the early 19th century. It is a review of an 1803 trial on a theft perpetrated against the company, its partners at the time being Charles Dixon Jr, James Brett and Aaron Morgan. A certain Timothy Tool, who was employed to assist in bottling port wine, was indicted for *felonious stealing* (larceny).[3] The method of buying barrels at their place of production, before commercialising at the end destination, including the bottling and labeling, had been in use for centuries. The vicissitudes of this unfortunate thief further inform us that the company had a warehouse for storing the barrels and bottling in the same street where its headquarters were based, which would certainly be a drawback if they needed to move.

At first, the main product of the firm was port, so that Portugal was its main commercial reference abroad. For example, when Charles Dixon Sr died in 1797 he was described as a "Portuguese merchant". Moreover, among the products they offered existed a *Dixon's Double Diamond*, a Port immortalised by Charles Dickens in his 1838 novel, *Nicholas Nickleby*, where the character Ned says to the butler: *"A magnum of the Double-*

---

[3]. The value of the stolen goods, five bottles and a gallon of wine, was 15 pennies for the bottles and 18 shillings for the wine. Tool was confined for three months at Newgate Prison and publicly whipped.

Diamond, David, to drink the health of Mr Linkinwater".[4]

Both Charles Dixon Jr and Aaron Morgan amassed a huge fortune, but their lives ultimately differed. While Dixon finally left the business, Morgan focused on providing an important legacy to his descendants. Together with his wife Margaret, born in 1742, they raised a large family, though only one son and three daughters reached adulthood, while seven children died in infancy. Their daughters, Maria, Jane Elizabeth and Edith, had different destinies, while their son, Thomas, became a partner and, later, heir to the business.

Maria Morgan, who was born in 1783, married John Sykes, captain of the East India Company. Their marriage led her to India, where Maria and her husband witnessed the local customs. She compiled her experiences in a memoir that has been used as a source in several historical works. Their marriage was brief, as Captain Sykes died in 1815, just seven years after their wedding; nevertheless, they had two daughters and a son.

Jane Elizabeth, born in 1788, married John Beevor of Chelsea. The couple had seven children; the eldest four were born in England and the three youngest in Tasmania. A few years after the death of Aaron Morgan, and possibly with the idea of starting a new life with his inheritance, they decided to leave England. Thus, in March 1821 the family arrived in Van Diemen's Land (Tasmania) on the ship *Emerald*. It is known that in 1822 John Peevor participated in the creation of an agricultural society, and that he bought a farm in the Coal River Valley, although it seems that, over the years, most of his children settled in Victoria, southern Australia.

There is little data on Edith, who appears to have been the youngest of Aaron Morgan's daughters. She married a man named Christopher Harrison in 1814, and it seems that they had no children.

Thomas Morgan was, as noted above, the business heir of Aaron Morgan. Married to Elizabeth Bonney in April 1818, his role in the history of the family business was also crucial, as his management coincided with the departure of Dixon, as well as with a diversification process that would later involve his children.

At this point, it is interesting to highlight some personal aspects of the life of Aaron Morgan and his descendants. Perhaps one of the most important is his link with Southwark and nearby areas of London, crossing the river in the zone of the Tower of London, where the firm's headquarters were situated, and south of the Thames, especially at Dulwich, where Aaron had his residence.

In particular, his bond with the parishes of the area, primarily St Olave and St Saviour (now Southwark Cathedral) is a fact to emphasise. St Olave

---

4. Charles Dickens, *Nicholas Nickleby*, Penguin Classics, London, 1999, Chapter xxxvii, p. 499.

is very close to Savage Gardens (just one street away) and witnessed many of the Morgan family's religious events, such as the weddings of Jane Elizabeth, Edith, and Thomas Morgan. In the latter case, a window with the names and symbols of the Morgan (a *griffin segreant sable*) and Bonney (three *fleurs-de-lys*) families, recalls their marriage.

However, Aaron Morgan should be linked more closely to St Saviour, the former parish of St Mary Overy and, since 1905, Southwark Cathedral. Together with Matthew Concanen, Aaron Morgan wrote *The History and Antiquities of the Parish of St Saviour's*, a book published in 1795 that describes the history of both the neighbourhood and the church.

Furthermore, he was buried there beside his wife, who died of apoplexy several years before him. His participation in the book quoted above probably had some influence on him receiving this honour. There is also a commemorative monument there, consisting of a fine tablet with ornamental pilasters and a bust of him, made by sculptor Thomas Cooke, inscribed:

> SACRED
> to the Memory of
> AARON MORGAN Esq[re]
> late of Savage Gardens, London,
> who died at Dulwich the 13th of October 1818
> in the 71st Year of his Age.
> He was many Years an Inhabitant of this Parish
> and one of the Authors of its History and Antiquities.
> Also of MARGARET MORGAN, Wife of the above
> who died the 31st of October 1810, aged 68 Years.
> Their mortal Remains are deposited in the Family Vault in the Middle Aisle:
> and near them Seven of their Children,
> who died in infancy.

Indeed, Aaron Morgan died in Dulwich on October 13th 1818, only a few months after the marriage of his son Thomas (April 24th), already a partner of the firm, and sole executor of his will. Thomas took over the management of the company, and he ran it until well into the 19th century.

Over the years, the firm, which had been specialising in port, began to diversify into various wines such as sherry, red wine, Claret, Madeira, and others. This fact implied the development of an extensive commercial network and an intricate system of international relations.[5] Existing archives related to its business operations reflect a considerable complexity, given the

---

5. For example, in a curious link, John James Ruskin's correspondence addressed to Thomas Morgan is preserved. Ruskin was a major partner of Ruskin, Telford & Domecq (exporters of sherry), father of the prominent Victorian writer John Ruskin, whose influence on Tolkien has been highlighted by some authors. For example, Patrick Curry says that, "If Middle-earth had a prophet, he was John Ruskin". P. Curry, *Defending Middle-earth: Tolkien, myth and modernity*, Floris Books, Edinburgh, 1997, p. 132.

substantial amounts of money handled and the large list of companies that dealt with the firm.

In the decade of the 1820's, Thomas Morgan's children were born: Thomas (1820), Francis (1821) and Aaron Augustus (1822). Thomas Jr and Francis were involved with the firm, but Aaron Augustus was called to religious life and was ordained an Anglican priest.

The company faced changes from the 1830's onwards, coinciding with the boys' growth. In 1835 Charles Dixon Jr left the firm, bought a large estate in Sussex (including a grand house called Stansted Park), and devoted himself to social life and prestigious occupations such as High Sheriff of Sussex. In 1840, the company changed its name to Thomas Morgan & Co., and its headquarters moved to 11 Mark Lane, very near to Savage Gardens. However, in 1845, under the name Morgan Jun. & Ridge, they returned to this latter street, specifically to number 24, and remained there until 1865.

A significant change happened during the 1840's as the business diversified, with special emphasis given to the trade of sherry. Although the company already sold this drink, it was now conditioned by the distance to southern Spain, the place of its production and primary distribution point.

Javier Maldonado Rosso, a great expert on the subject, explains the evolution of the sherry industry and states three different generations of distributors of sherry, between the 18th and 19th centuries, to the British market. The first period covers until the end of the Napoleonic wars and refers to the British pioneers who arrived in Spain in the period between these two centuries and, in many cases accidentally, founded or acquired wineries and export houses. A second generation, until the fourth decade of the 19th century, stimulated the business with the spectacular growth of exports from local wines to the British market and an increasing number of companies dedicated to wine storage. Finally, in a third phase:

> The continued expansion of sherry in the British market created huge demands among some British merchants so that it seems they set out to conquer the production centres of sherry, to control the business from its early stages. Such were the cases of Perkins and Bradley, and of Allen, Morgan and Co. These British merchants were at first wholesalers in England, and bought wine from different British agents from the export houses of Jerez de la Frontera and Port St Mary for its subsequent distribution through the networks they had woven in that country. In this period, however, they resolved not only to skip this second step of the process in which they were becoming agents of sherry trade houses, but they settled in the area as export houses in their own right.[6]

---

6. Javier Maldonado Rosso, *La formación del capitalismo en el marco de Jerez: De la vitivinicultura tradicional a la agroindustria vinatera moderna (siglos XVII y XIX)*, Huerga y Fierro Editores, 1999, p. 263. (Translated by the author of this work).

So, as a first step in the development of this third phase, Allen, Morgan and Co. was established in 1841 in partnership with John Allen (a prominent liquor dealer established in Porto). The firm set up a headquarter in Port St Mary (Spain) in the "Shire of the sherry". As Morgan's representative, his second son, Francis, moved to Spain.

With Thomas Morgan and, later, Thomas Jr managing the business from London, Francis Morgan was responsible for creating the network of production and exportation in Spain needed to avoid intermediaries. Although Allen & Morgan went into liquidation in 1847 (to Morgan Jr & Ridge), Francis Morgan stayed in Spain and became a crucial link to his family business and, above all, established his own ties. Our story continues with him because, even though he initially resided in Spain temporarily, he settled there permanently after his marriage to María Manuela Osborne and, in fact, one of his sons is the subject of this work.

As for the lives of Thomas Jr and Aaron Augustus, Thomas, although dedicated to the wine merchant business, had a deep passion (apparently shared by other family members) for archaeology. In fact, he was a member of the British Archaeological Association since his youth and, given his experience in accounting matters, he became treasurer and, subsequently, vice-president and honorary treasurer. He cultivated his hobby until his death in 1892 and was the author of several articles. He even published a book of some significance: *Romano-British mosaic pavements; a history of their discovery, and a record and interpretation of their designs*.

Thomas Jr took up residence in Lamberth, not too far from Dulwich, and had a large family. His sons, Albert Charles Frederick and Ernest Kennedy Buckley, shared his love for archaeology, becoming members of the British Archaeological Association. Albert would continue in the family business, however, with Ernest joining the Anglican priesthood. Albert moved to Portugal, in Vila Nova de Gaia, a town right in front of Porto, separated only by the Douro river, and married Marian Fladgate, daughter of John Alexander Fladgate, of Taylor, Fladgate & Co., one of the leading traders in Porto. Similarly, James, son of Ernest, also moved to Portugal, and both played a similar role to that of Francis Morgan in Spain. Other children of Thomas Jr, such as Aaron Herbert, continued the business from England.

After his studies at St John's College, in Cambridge, Aaron Augustus Morgan was ordained a member of the Anglican clergy and brought his ministry to various places in the United Kingdom, including as a military chaplain during the Crimean War. He died at Tivoli, near Rome, in 1888. He is the author of two interesting works: *The Mind of Shakespeare*, about the author himself, and also a translation of *Ecclesiastes*.

The Böhl de Faber Family

The parents of María Manuela Osborne Böhl de Faber were Thomas Osborne-Mann and Aurora Böhl de Faber. Osborne-Mann was a wine merchant from southern England, while Aurora was the second daughter of Juan Nicolás Böhl de Faber[1] and Francisca Ruiz de Larrea (better known as Frasquita Larrea). Aurora's older sister was Cecilia Böhl de Faber, the famous writer more commonly known by her masculine pseudonym, Fernán Caballero.

Juan Nicolás Böhl de Faber and Frasquita Larrea are one of the most intellectually stimulating married couples of early 19th century Spain. He was born on December 9th 1770, and was the eldest of five children by Johann Jacob Böhl, a Hamburg merchant who belonged to the gentry. Juan Nicolás was particularly attached to his younger brother Antonio Amadeo (Anton Gottlieb), born in 1772, with whom he shared education and duties in the management of the business delegation founded by their father in Cadiz, dedicated to the trade of Silesia fabric.

They were born into the Lutheran religion, and their tutor was the famous German writer and pedagogue, Joachim Heinrich Campe, who provided them with a good education. Campe, a follower of the ideas of Rousseau, also dealt with the education of other famous people, like the Humboldt brothers. In fact, years later, Wilhelm von Humboldt[2] would travel to Cadiz as a guest of Juan Nicolás.

Profound and lasting bonds of affection were established between the Campe family (Joachim Heinrich and his wife) and Juan Nicolás, to the point where he came to refer to them as his adoptive parents and maintained, in particular with Campe's niece, Elise, a long and fruitful correspondence. Perhaps the definitive proof of this link between tutor and student can be found in Campe's most famous book, *Robinson der Jüngere*, which tells the story of a boy on a deserted island, where the protagonist, named Johannes,

---

1. As with other cases, his hispanicised name will be used in this work because he employed it in Spain, although he was called Johann Niklaus Böhl von Faber in his native German.
2. Wilhelm (1767-1835) and Alexander (1769-1859) von Humboldt (the better known of the two), are one of the most famous pairs of brothers of their times. Both were born in Berlin, to an upper-class family, his father being a senior official of Wilhelm II. They received an excellent education and their lives coincided with an era largely conditioned by the consequences of the French Revolution. Both are remembered for their influence in the areas where they developed their careers. Wilhelm was devoted to politics and public administration, but was also an outstanding poet and philologist (specializing in comparative philology). On the other hand, Alexander is considered one of the greatest naturalists of all time. Throughout his life, he travelled around the world making numerous discoveries, and becoming a great defender of the scientific method.

was inspired by Juan Nicolás.

After a period of study in England, Juan Nicolás arrived in Cadiz at the age of fifteen, ready to take over the family business, and was joined shortly after by his brother. The latter would go on to show greater commercial ability, while Juan Nicolás was reluctant to take care of business and was instead inclined towards his growing literary and intellectual concerns. Their ordinary life in this period was altered by the death of their father and the subsequent marriage of their mother to Martin Jacob von Faber, which gave both brothers not only a second surname but also an improvement in their peerage.

Juan Nicolás married Josefa Francisca Xaviera Josefa Gregoria Ruiz de Larrea y Aherán, better known as Frasquita Larrea, on February 1st 1796. The union would lead to a complex personal and intellectual relationship, even before their marriage, which had to overcome problems arising from religious differences, as Frasquita was Catholic and Juan Nicolás Protestant.

He describes Frasquita, in a letter dated from 1797 to Elise Campe, as *"very dark, with abundant brown hair, pretty eyes, beautiful eyebrows, and big ugly nose, big mouth with red lips and healthy teeth. She has a good disposition for everything, but her culture is hampered by some strongly held romantic ideas"*.[3]

Frasquita Larrea was the only child from the marriage between a Basque nobleman called Antonio Ruiz de Larrea, born in Mendiola near Vitoria (although his family came from Zuazo, also in Alava), established in Cadiz in the mid-eighteenth century, and Francisca Xaviera Aherán y Molonny, of Irish origin. Frasquita received an excellent education in France and England, and she developed a romantic personality (as her husband indicated) curiously combined with feelings which, in a way, could be described as feminist in the context of her time. Indeed, E. Herman Hespelt noted her "desire to take part in the intellectual and political life of her time".[4]

Their marriage began with a long trip to Germany, with Frasquita's mother. Their eldest daughter, Cecilia (who eventually would become a well-known writer under the pseudonym Fernán Caballero)[5], was born in

---

3. Elisabeth Campe, *Versuch einer Lebensskizze von Johan Nikolas Böhl von Faber. Nach seinen eigenen Briefen*, Als Handschrift gedruckt, Brockhaus, Leipzig, 1858, p. 38.
4. E.Herman Hespelt, *Francisca de Larrea, a Spanish Feminist of the early Nineteenth Century*, Hispania XIII, 3 (May 1930), pp. 173-186.
5. Cecilia Böhl de Faber (1796-1877), who used the *nom de plume* Fernán Caballero, is one of the main female Spanish writers of the 19th century (and possibly of all time) and, without doubt, the most widely translated. Regarding her works, she is the foremost representative author of modern Spanish novels on customs: the *costumbrism*. She describes, through a moralistic and naive prism, habits, traditions and different typologies from the society of her time, especially inside Andalusian society. One of her main literary interests was, in fact, recovery of the traditional folklore. Her main novel was *La Gaviota* (translated as *The Seagull*) but also of interest are *Clemencia, La familia Alvareda, Un servilón y un liberalito, El Alcázar de Sevilla, Una en otra, Elia, Lágrimas, Callar en vida y perdonar en muerte, Cuentos populares andaluces, Más largo es el tiempo que la fortuna, Un verano en Bornos, Cosa

Switzerland a few months later.

Back in Spain, Juan Nicolás had to manage the business alone after his brother's death as a result of the bubonic plague that devastated Cadiz. In this city, over a period of four years, their three other children were born: Aurora first, in 1799, Juan Jacobo (Johann Jakob), the only male child next, in 1800, and finally Ángela in 1803.

These were also the years of the famous *tertulias*[6], organised by Frasquita, which allowed her to connect with many prominent figures of the time. One such person was Blanco White[7] who, despite their ideological differences, she developed a long friendship with. These *tertulias* achieved great popularity and are cited by Pérez Galdós in his *National Episodes*[8], specifically in the episode *Cadiz*, where he compares them with the *tertulias* of liberal ideology organised by Doña Margarita López de Morla (who is called Doña Flora by Galdós):

> "We must defend freedom even in the *tertulias*" – said a bishop, or a dandy, I do not remember this well.
> "In the trenches is better," said Doña Flora. "I do not want to quarrel with Paquita Larrea, but if she receives Valiente, Ostolaza, Teneyro, Morro and Borrull, I can have the pleasure of having Argüelles, Toreno and Quintana in my house, not because I have chosen them among the liberals, but because they agree in their ideas."
> [...]
> I must point out that Doña Francisca Larrea, wife of the knowledgeable and worthy German Böhl de Faber, was a writer of much understanding, like her husband, who was very familiar with mastery of the Spanish language. From this marriage, Eliseo Böhl[9] was born, to whom we owe thanks for the best and most beautiful paintings on the customs of Andalusia, and who was also an unsurpassed novelist, whose fame is as great as it is well-deserved, in and

---

cumplida sólo en la otra vida: Diálogos entre la juventud y la edad madura, La farisea, etc.
6. Social gatherings with literary or artistic overtones.
7. José María Blanco y Crespo (1775-1851), called Joseph Blanco White, was the son of the English vice-consul in Seville. He was ordained a Catholic priest and served as canon in Cadiz and Seville. After his stay in these cities, he went to Madrid at the time of the French invasion of Spain during the Napoleonic period, and his struggle against the occupiers was significant. In 1810, after a spiritual conflict due to religious doubts, he travelled to England, where he remained until his death. There he became friends with several intellectuals from the University of Oxford, a place where he struck up a warm friendship with the future Cardinal, Newman (then still a member of the Anglican Church). White took Anglican orders, anglicised his name, and developed several literary and journalistic works characterised by fierce attacks on Spain and everything Spanish.
8. *The National Episodes* are probably the most recognised historical novels from the "father of modern Spanish realism", Benito Pérez Galdós (1843-1920). There are five series of historical stories that focus on specific moments in Spanish history, between the reign of Carlos IV and the time of the Restoration, contemporary to Galdós, and important landmarks in the 19th century Spanish narrative. Aside from the *National Episodes*, Galdós wrote other famous books, such as *Doña Perfecta, Maríanela, La familia de León Roch*, and *La Desheredada* and, among others, *Fortunata y Jacinta*.
9. Galdós's reference to Eliseo Böhl obviously corresponds to Cecilia Böhl de Faber.

outside of Spain.[10]

Juan Nicolás, his wife, his eldest daughter Cecilia, and his son Juan Jacobo, returned to Germany in 1805 to buy an estate and settle there. His other two daughters, Aurora and Ángela, stayed in Chiclana, near Cadiz, with his mother-in-law. Despite acquiring an estate in Mecklenburg, the cohabitation failed and Frasquita abandoned him in the spring of 1806 to return to Spain. The separation lasted until 1812, when Frasquita came back to Germany with their younger daughters (after having spent some time in England during the last months of her mother's life). The following year, several factors (including Juan Nicolás' debts, which caused the loss of his German estate, and his conversion to Catholicism) were triggers for their reconciliation, which culminated in their return to Spain.

While they were separated, Frasquita had witnessed the siege of Cadiz, some of the major events of the War of Independence in Spain, and the impact of the Napoleonic wars in Europe during the perilous journey of the year 1812. During this period, she developed patriotic feelings, as reflected in many of her letters and writings, which reinforced her opinion about the nobility of ideals stemming from ordinary people.[11]

Their family's return to Spain coincided with a time of economic hardship, especially from 1815, when the family business finally went bankrupt. However, this was also a fruitful period of creation, with Frasquita's translations of Chateaubriand and Lord Byron, as well as her own works. She wrote the stories of her travels to Bornos, Ubrique and Arcos de la Frontera, wherein she emphasised descriptions of the landscape, and the idea of peasantry being the bearer of integrity and virtue.

Meanwhile, Juan Nicolás was immersed in an intellectual debate with

---

10. Benito Pérez Galdós, *Guerra de la independencia. Tomo II. (Episodios Nacionales)*, Algaba Ediciones, Madrid, 2008, p. 312. (Translated by the author of this work).
11. Napoleon long considered Spain as a useful ally. However, its military weakness, as a result of the destruction of the Spanish fleet at Trafalgar, combined with conflicts in the royal succession, caused him to invade the country and replace the Spanish monarchy with a government headed by a member of his own family, his brother Joseph. With this move, Napoleon only considered the weakness of the Spanish monarchy, overlooking the reaction of the Spanish people. There was a popular uprising on May 2nd 1808, which began the so-called War of Independence, fundamentally a *guerrilla war*, between 1808 and 1814. Guerilla warfare was the only viable military strategy capable of counteracting the powerful Napoleonic army, and it ruled out the option of acting through conventional means. It was an armed movement of popular participation where the components of each *partida*, or armed unit, could be drawn from the regular army, or even from farmers, or bandits. Some leaders, like Juan Martín *El Empecinado*, Espoz y Mina, and El Cura Merino, became heroes. During the war, the French also fought against the English forces commanded by the Duke of Wellington, which helped the Spanish to expel the French in 1814. The Spanish War of Independence was the first of the wars of national liberation in which the Napoleonic Empire was defeated, and it had enormous resonance for the rest of Europe. In the literary field, the conflict brought the seed of the Romantic movement to Spain, arousing a desire for freedom, which was a distinctly romantic theme. The contemporary translations of works such as the ones from Lord Byron, Goethe and Chateaubriand into Spanish also had a significant influence.

Alcalá Galiano and José Joaquín de Mora. Juan Nicolás claimed vindication of his ideals, which were conservative, and even reactionary, in their nature. They were typical of what would later be called Spanish Historical Romanticism, exalting the alleged particularity of the Spanish spirit, and the glories of the past, against the Enlightenment and its rational nature. It has in fact been said that Romanticism was introduced in Spain as a result of the Böhl de Faber marriage.

The economic situation improved when, around 1820, Juan Nicolás began working for the winery Duff-Gordon. Privately, he quipped about his fate, which had led him to become a "cognac dealer". However, the family soon achieved a prosperity that allowed his daughters to have good marriages and, from the point of view of his intellectual curiosity, he was free to pursue his literary disposition. Able to acquire new books, he formed a great library. In this period, his merits as an illustrious Hispanophile were also recognised, with his admission to the Royal Spanish Academy.

In the early twenties, the company Duff-Gordon relocated to Port St Mary, along with Juan Nicolás, Frasquita, and the rest of the family, except for their son, who settled in Germany. Their last years were not spent in good health: Frasquita showed visible symptoms of neurasthenia, and Juan Nicolás' health worsened, likely because of diabetes. He died on November 9th 1836, followed by Frasquita just two years later, on September 14th 1838.

From Duff-Gordon to Osborne

Aurora, the second daughter of the Böhl de Faber union, has only briefly been mentioned in the previous chapter. In a way, she was eclipsed by her parents and sister, since she played the role of wife, mother and grandmother, away from the intellectual interests and business affairs. However, thanks to letters and descriptions from her immediate family, a fairly accurate picture of her life can be composed.

María de la Aurora Josefa Rosalía Canuta Böhl de Faber y Ruiz de Larrea was born in Cadiz on January 19th 1799. She was just two years younger than her sister Cecilia, and her childhood coincided with the separation of her parents. She stayed with her mother and her sister Ángela, while Cecilia and her brother, Juan Jacobo, remained in Germany with her father. Although her early years were spent in Cadiz, she also later resided in the small town of Chiclana with her mother and grandmother.

Between late 1811 and 1813, Aurora travelled with her mother to Germany, via England and France, from where the whole family, except for her brother, returned to Spain. This trip was certainly an odyssey for Aurora and her younger sister Ángela, who was around ten years old. They witnessed the death of their maternal grandmother and the chaos caused by the war in Europe.

After the long journey, the family returned to Cadiz. In this period, in 1816, when she was just seventeen years old, her father describes Aurora in a letter to Campe's wife as follows: "The second daughter, Aurora, is a gentle and lovely girl, although she is somewhat of delicate health, which gives us concern". Her youthful character was remarkably cheerful, to the point where, elsewhere, she is described as "a girl of almost irresponsible joy".[1]

Shorly after, Juan Nicolás began working for Duff-Gordon, and the family overcame its financial problems. At that time, Aurora received a marriage proposal. Despite the timid objections of her mother about her suitor, probably due to the age difference, she eventually received the full approval of both her parents and became the only one of their daughters to give them grandchildren.

Her sisters' marriages proved to be more troubled. Cecilia married three times. The first time appears to have been a youthful moment of madness

---

1. Elisabeth Campe, *Versuch einer Lebensskizze von Johan Nikolas Böhl von Faber. Nach seinen eigenen Briefen*, Als Handschrift gedruckt, Brockhaus, Leipzig, 1858, p. 85.

with a young army captain who died soon after; next was the Marquis of Arco Hermoso, who seems to have made her happy until his premature death; lastly, she married a young man named Antonio Arrom, of few possessions, who finally committed suicide.

Her younger sister Ángela, who had a defect in her hip from youth that made her limp, married Baron Chatry de La Fosse, a French general. He was described by Frasquita Larrea as "old, Protestant, sick and a womaniser". He was much older than Ángela, who was only twenty years old when they married, and a Jacobin, afflicted by, among other maladies, incontinence. They lived for extended periods in Paris until the general's death in 1848. She then married Fermín Iribarren, brother of the Marquis of Villarreal and Purullena, who was a friend of her sister, Cecilia.

Neither Cecilia nor Ángela had children. Their brother, Juan Jacobo, by contrast, had eight children, but he lived in Germany and so his family connections with Spain were less close.

Aurora was married at the Iglesia Prioral of Port St Mary on November 12th 1825, to Thomas Osborne-Mann, who was an important partner in Duff-Gordon. He was a respectable and ambitious businessman, and arguably the opposite of Juan Nicolás Böhl de Faber, given his innate commercial aptitude.

Thomas Osborne-Mann came from Devon, in England, where he was born in 1781. His family belonged to the small English gentry who, from at least the mid-sixteenth century, had lived in the area of Paignton, where they owned an estate. Today, Paignton is a major tourist city near Torquay, and part of the so-called "English Riviera". Until the 19th century, it was a fishing town, and the principal wealth of its hamlets, such as Stoke Gabriel (a place where many members of the Osborne family were natives), came from agriculture, and especially from fruit and cider.

Thomas' father, the Rev. Peter Osborne, took over the family estate at Paignton, and added other lands to this (which he acquired during his life, improving the family's legacy). These new lands were north of Paignton, near the city of Exeter. The heir to all these properties was Thomas' older brother, also called Peter, who had studied at Exeter College in Oxford and became a church minister. Peter married Charlotte Shore, eldest daughter of Lord Shore, who was the First Baron of Teignmouth, an official in the East India Company and, subsequently, Governor-General of India from 1793 to 1797.

Thomas arrived in Spain in the early 19th century (although, according to other sources, it was in the late 18th century). He was probably in search of fortune, seeing as, on the one hand, his family legacy had passed to his brother and, on the other, the area of Cadiz offered great trading opportunities. When Peter died childless, in 1850, Thomas inherited the family estate.

He converted to Catholicism in Cadiz, where he joined Lornegan and White, a leading firm of bankers and traders. As an associate, he began to develop his own export agency, before partnering with Daniel Macpherson, who traded in various products, such as sugar, spices and tobacco.

Soon he became acquainted with Sir James Duff, the British Consul in Cadiz, and his nephew William Gordon, who in 1772 had founded a pioneer house for the production and export of wines, called Duff-Gordon. James Duff was a bachelor, and his nephew William (his sister Ann's son) became his heir. Now associated to Duff-Gordon, Thomas Osborne-Mann played a significant role in the firm. In the early 19th century, James Duff had grown old; his nephew William was no longer able to manage the company, as he was a member of the Parliament that had been representing Worcester since 1807, and spent his time in England. Thus, upon his uncle's death in 1815, he inherited the baronetcy and changed his surname from Gordon to Duff-Gordon.

Thomas Osborne-Mann and Aurora had a solid family life; their wealth quickly grew, and they were blessed with many children. Firstly, three daughters were born: María Manuela in 1827, Cecilia in 1831 and Francisca Xaviera in 1833. They then had a couple of sons: Tomás, in 1836, and Juan Nicolás, who was born two years later. Juan Nicolás' godmother was his older sister, María Manuela.

The couple's children were educated in England, so beginning a lasting tradition among the Osborne family members. Born before the establishment of Catholic public schools in England, they were sent to Newark-on-Trent, where the erudite priest James Waterworth ran a school for the children of prominent British Catholic families.

The Osbornes were bilingual, both for sentimental reasons and for practical business concerns. They chose an English education, but kept their dual citizenship even though, in terms of lifestyle and habits, they preferred their Spanish heritage. This sentiment is supported by the hispanisation of their names, as is especially reflected in the case of their firstborn son, Tomás (spelt significantly without the letter "h" present and with an accented "a").

Thomas Osborne-Mann adored his wife, and she made him very happy. For him, a mature man when he married, Aurora must have seemed like an angel who satisfied all his yearnings and gave him healthy children. Indeed, their children were the joy of the whole family, including their aunts and grandparents. This was despite the fact that Tomás, the eldest son, was barely a few months old when his grandfather, Juan Nicolás Böhl de Faber, died. Their presence brought great happiness even during this time of grief.

Cecilia Böhl de Faber provides us with ample example of the warmth that was felt for Thomas' children, in particular towards the boys. She corresponded affectionately with them all her life. She did also get along with her nieces, though she had some problems with them (and their husbands).

The Osborne house was wealthy and well-frequented, with illustrious guests usually present there. One of the most prominent visitors was the American writer Washington Irving, who befriended several members of the family, including Juan Nicolás Böhl de Faber and his daughter Cecilia. He was particularly friendly with Thomas Osborne-Mann, not least because of Irving's great love for sherry.

Irving, who was born in New York in 1783, travelled to Port St Mary during his first stay in Spain. After the death of his mother, he had decided to remain in Europe for an extended period. He was in Spain towards the end of the 1820s, researching his biography of Columbus, but also writing and travelling around the country (especially Andalusia), which allowed him to interact with many Spanish personalities of the time.

Port St Mary was one of his destinations. There, he developed a close relationship with the Osborne family, and it is said that he completed one of his masterpieces, *Tales of the Alhambra*, at one of the family estates, *El Cerrillo*. His relationship with them continued for many years, and Irving took on the role of ambassador of the sherry trade for America. In fact, he popularised the *Sherry Cobbler* in New York, a cocktail made from sherry, water, lemon and sugar.

Anecdotes aside, nothing distracted Thomas Osborne-Mann from his work and, thanks to his efforts, the company grew both in productivity (initially, the primary focus of business was its commercialisation) and sales (among the top customers were several royal houses). When he died in Port St Mary, on February 16th 1854, he left considerable wealth and a prosperous business which endures even today.

His wife Aurora lived a further fifteen years after his death and became the happy matriarch of the family, surrounded by her numerous grandchildren. However, she also faced family rifts caused by the confrontations among her sons-in-law and her sister Cecilia, where she again showed proof of her good nature. Cecilia was in a difficult economic situation (mainly due to the disastrous administration of her goods by her husband, Antonio Arrom), and often clashed with the spouses of Aurora's daughters, Cecilia and Paca (Francisca Xaviera). They were important marquises, who blackmailed and forced Cecilia and her husband to leave Port St Mary in order to avoid discomfort and ridicule.

During this period, Aurora had to maintain her sister and her brother-in-law. Years later, Cecilia Böhl de Faber wrote to Tomás, the eldest son of Aurora, about this and told how his mother gave her an ounce of gold monthly, while her young husband tried to succeed in business and a diplomatic career as consul of Spain in Australia:

I only received one ounce per month, thanks to the charity of your good mother, although your uncle stipulated as a condition to leave a payment for me of an ounce until he began to earn a salary [...] what an outrage for a woman such as me, sister of Aurora, the mother of their wives, widow of the owner of everything.[2]

Aurora's last years were marked by health problems. By 1868, a lump had appeared on her breast, a symptom of the cancer which would be diagnosed in Paris. After some months of uncertainty and suffering in the French capital, being treated by doctors as illustrious as Auguste Nélaton, Aurora finally decided not to have surgery, and returned home. There, at Port St Mary, her agony finally ended on February 1st 1869. She died in the presence of her five children.

The legacy left by the union between Thomas Osborne-Mann and Aurora Böhl de Faber goes far beyond their goods. Osborne-Mann built a great company but, most importantly, his family had been perfectly integrated into its environment and became a notable presence, especially in the social life of the region.

From an economic point of view, the Osborne family had bought the shares of Duff-Gordon in the mid-nineteenth century and taken full control of the company, which would later change its name to Osborne. The reason for this change was the introduction of its products into the Spanish market (before, they had been virtually restricted to the British market), which forced them to look for a name with a good sound that was easy to pronounce both in English and in Spanish.

To understand the loss of interest on the part of the Duff-Gordon heirs and consequent sale of their shares, it is interesting to analyse the attitude of the descendants of William Duff-Gordon (who was married in 1810 to Caroline Cornewall). His two sons had a relationship with the company that could be described, at best, as minimally committed, at least on the production side. Perhaps their social standing, as members of high society, and a particular disdain for commercial affairs, were significant reasons for this.

One of the brothers, Cosmo (Cosme in Spanish) Duff-Gordon, who was born in 1812, had a greater involvement in the company. He acted as its representative in England and witnessed Cecilia Böhl de Faber's varying fortunes during her trips to England (of particular mention is an event in 1836, when she was staying at his home and had to return suddenly to Spain due to Juan Nicolás Böhl de Faber's impending death). Cecilia, of course, was the daughter of a manager of the company.

---

2. Milagros Fernández Poza, *Frasquita Larrea y "Fernán Caballero" Mujer, revolución y romanticismo en España 1775-1870*, Biblioteca de Temas Portuenses, Ayto. El Puerto de Santa María, El Puerto de Santa María, 2001, p. 401. (Translated by the author of this work).

However, Cosmo left the business in 1857 (and, in 1872, recognised Tomás Osborne Böhl de Faber and his brother Juan Nicolás as sole shareholders of the company) to deal with other issues in his country, where he lived until his death in 1898. Curiously, his eldest son, who was also called Cosmo, would go down in history as one of the survivors of the Titanic.[3]

His brother, Alexander Duff-Gordon, was barely involved in the family business. In 1840, he married Lucy Austin, who would become the famous Lady Duff-Gordon, and they became one of the most popular couples in the London of the mid-nineteenth century. Their circle of friends included Dickens, Thackeray and Tennyson. She is remembered as the author of the famous travel book, *Letters from Egypt*, which describes the long journey the couple made to the Middle East.

The purchasing of the shares in the Duff-Gordon company and the change of ownership did not go unnoticed in British society. It even generated a little confusion, as revealed by the following fragment of a letter, dated August 1862, from (famous author, mother of Lady Duff-Gordon, and mother-in-law of Alexander Duff-Gordon) Sarah Austin's correspondence with John Linnell, a prominent Victorian painter:

August 20th 1862

Dear Mr Linnell,
I beg your pardon for so long delaying to answer your inquiry. The truth is that, in the hurry and agitation of my dear daughter's second departure (she starts today for the Pyrenees, and then Egypt) I entirely forgot it, which I am sure you will allow for. My son-in-law never had anything to do with the "Duff Gordon Sherry" trade, which, owing to his father's death, passed into other hands when he was a boy. His brother had a share in it for some years, but retired from it some years ago, and has now nothing to do with it. I fear, therefore, I can be of no service to you in the way you mention. I do not even know the names of the present successors to the business.[4]

---

3. Sir Cosmo Edmund Duff Gordon (1862-1931) inherited the title of Baron from his father. Member of the Great Britain Olympic fencing team at the Games of 1908, he has gone down in history as a survivor of the sinking of the RMS Titanic in 1912. He and his wife boarded a nearly empty lifeboat and were accused of bribing the crew not to return to rescue other passengers who were trying to survive in the icy waters. Although the couple were acquitted of any charges, their reputation suffered greatly. Curiously, they signed onto the ship as Mr and Mrs Morgan.
4. Alfred Thomas Story, *The Life of John Linnell*, Richard Bentley and Son, London, 1892, pp. 132-133.

The Wedding of María Manuela

Focusing on marriages, in every generation from Juan Nicolás Böhl de Faber and Frasquita Larrea, it seemed there was always someone in the family rebelling against the general consensus of opinions about the appropriateness of their chosen suitor. This was the case with Juan Nicolás and Frasquita, on religious grounds, and with both the first and third marriages of Cecilia Böhl de Faber, and with the first marriage of her sister, Ángela. The family's social position should have led to them becoming engaged to members of the aristocracy or the upper class (which their sister Aurora did, and eventually they did too in their second marriages).

In the generation that followed (for the purposes of this book, we will only consider Aurora's children and not those of her brother, Juan Jacobo, who lived in Germany), there was also a similar act of rebellion but, in this case, the results were unexpectedly satisfactory.

It is of note that three daughters and two sons resulted from the marriage between Osborne-Mann and Aurora. The daughters were María Manuela, Cecilia, and Francisca Xaviera, with total age difference between them of six years. The sons were much younger and were born during the last years of their father's life. At the time of his death, they hadn't yet come of age.

María Manuela, Fr. Francis Morgan's mother, was the eldest of these children, although this has limited relevance, because the *crucial* children with regards to business (and society also) were the male heirs. When she was twenty-two years old, she notified her parents of her desire to marry. Her sister Cecilia was already planning her marriage to the Marquis of Castilleja del Campo, and the youngest sister would shortly be married to the Marquis of Saltillo. The matter of María Manuela's marriage, rather than becoming an occasion for joy, was an unpleasant surprise for the whole family, given the suitor.

The Osborne family, who were traditionally Spanish in their social habits, relations and religion (they were, of course, Catholics), were baffled by Maria Manuela's desire to marry Francis Morgan. Yes, he was associated with the wine trade, but there were several other factors counting against him, especially in comparison to his soon-to-be brothers-in-law.

Even Cecilia Böhl de Faber wrote, in several letters, about everyone's astonishment, and of her own annoyance. In the extract below, dated June 15th 1849, she writes to the famous scholar, and friend of the family, Eugenio

Hartzenbusch:

> María Manuela is getting married, against the wishes of the family, to an Englishman. When parents are as permissive as my sister is, this is what they get in return... Poor Aurora, a Protestant![1]

Interestingly, her best known work, titled *The Seagull*, was published in the same year. In this novel, there is a scene with obvious parallels, but with a different conclusion: a female character rejects, for religious reasons, a marriage offer from an important Englishman:

> "But the best has yet to come," continued Rafael, fixing his eyes on a pretty girl who was sitting by the marchioness, watching her play at cards. "Sir John is desperately in love with my cousin Rita, and has made her an offer. Rita, who absolutely doesn't know how to pronounce the monosyllable "Yes," gave him a "No," as short and sharp as a cannon-shot".
> "Is it possible, Rita," asked the duke, "that you have refused twenty thousand a-year?"
> "I didn't refuse the income," replied the young girl, coolly, without lifting her eyes from the game. "What I refused was its owner."
> "You did well," said the general; "everyone should marry in his own country, then cats are not mistaken for hares."
> "You did well, indeed," added the marchioness. "A Protestant! God forbid!"
> "And what do you say, countess?" asked the duke.
> "I agree with my mother," she replied. "It is no joking matter, when the husband is of a different religion from his wife. I think, with my uncle, that every one should marry in his own country, and I agree with Rita, that I would never marry a man only because he had twenty thousand a-year."[2]

At that time, in order to celebrate a marriage between a Protestant and a Catholic, it was necessary to obtain a papal dispensation. Such a document could only be issued by the ecclesiastical authorities and, ultimately, by the Pope himself. The criteria, traditions and norms usually applied to these issues, were compiled in 1917 in the first Code of Canon Law, a comprehensive legislative and legal system of the Catholic Church, which included worldly and religious matters. Under this code, dispensations for mixed-religion marriages were granted only if there was a prior commitment, made in writing by both spouses, to baptise and educate children in the Catholic Church; at the same time, the non-Catholic spouse would commit to avoiding any perversion of the Catholic partner's faith. In turn, the Catholic spouse was encouraged to prudently attempt to convert their partner.

---

1. Theodor Heinerman, *Cecilia Böhl de Faber y Juan Eugenio Hartzenbusch, una correspondencia inédita*, Espasa Calpe, Madrid, 1944, p. 89. (Translated by the author of this work).
2. Fernán Caballero, *The Seagull*, Richard Bentley, New Burlington Street, London, 1867, pp. 288-289.

Indeed, this agreement explains why all of their children were educated in the Catholic faith. In any case, María Manuela was not *perverted*; that is, converted to Anglicanism. On the other hand, how much pressure she exerted in trying to convert her husband is unknown, but the fact is that he retained his faith all his life.

In 1849, when the dispensation was requested, the Catholic Church was ruled by Pope Pius IX who, due to the unstable political climate (at that time, the Pope accrued temporal power over large areas of the incipient Italy), had to flee Rome in November 1848. Although the situation was restored a few months later with the help of the French army, the Pope would not return to the Vatican until April 1850.

This extraordinary situation delayed the couple's plans and caused some distress among the family members. In another letter addressed, again, to Hartzenbusch, dated February 1850, Cecilia Böhl de Faber expressed her displeasure:

> María Manuela, the brunette, is not married, because the Pope gives as little urgency to granting the license as he does to returning to Rome.[3]

At last, their wedding took place on February 3rd 1851, but with two singular aspects: it was held in the United Kingdom, and was officiated in both Anglican and Catholic rites. In addition, it wasn't hugely attended, at least from the Spanish side of the family, and featured the noteworthy absence of the father of the bride.

> Aurora took María Manuela to England to marry there because she, being English, enjoys this prerogative. Osborne is rejuvenated. Cecilia, who is raising a beautiful boy named Antonio, and Ángela, are well. Everybody wishes for me to pass a thousand affections to you.[4]

Newark-on-Trent, in Nottinghamshire, a town of 11,330 inhabitants, and famous for its beer production, was the chosen place for this celebration. The Anglican ceremony was held at the Church of St Mary Magdalene, one of the finest parish churches in the country. Its impressive tower (the fifth highest in England) is its most notable feature, although four different architectural styles, dating back to the medieval period, can be found in this church.

Precisely at the time of the wedding, the Church was undergoing a major restoration, at the instigation of the Vicar John Garrett Bussell. The most important interventions were the reconstruction of the organ and the

---
3. Op. cit. [1], p. 115.
4. Op. cit., p. 126.

replacement of an altarpiece, which featured a representation of the raising of Lazarus, included within a set of scenes from the life of Mary Magdalene. The ceremony was officiated by another reverend, Aaron Augustus Morgan, the groom's brother, who has already been mentioned. He was ordained in 1846 and, from then until 1855, was appointed to the rectory of Bradley, Lincolnshire, fifty miles from Newark. Regarding the Catholic wedding, the celebrant was James Waterworth, a learned priest residing in the city, who also ran a private Catholic school which María Manuela and her brothers had attended several years earlier.

The wedding was followed by a honeymoon, also in England. They spent part of it at a particularly unique place, which gives us an idea of the good relations and high standing of the newlyweds' families. This place was the magnificent Aston Hall mansion, in Birmingham.

During the 18th and 19th centuries, Birmingham experienced a long process of industrial growth which provoked an expansion of the city, and the subsequent incorporation of nearby rural areas. A good example of one such area was Aston, whose most notable reference was the aforementioned Aston Hall, a grand house surrounded by beautiful gardens. It was built between 1618 and 1635 by Sir Thomas Holte, and belonged to his family until around 1817. It was acquired by James Watt Jr (eldest son of the famous instrument maker, and inventor of the steam machine, James Watt), who possessed great wealth, gained in the era of industrial development. He continued on his father's path, establishing the world's first complete machine manufacturing factory.

James Watt Jr lived in Aston Hall until his death in 1848. Not too many details are known about their owners until 1858, when the property was acquired by a company seeking to open Aston Hall as a public park and museum, although it finally passed into municipal ownership in 1864. It seems that, when Watt died, Aston Hall returned to the Holte family, who were acquaintances of the Morgans. Specifically, it returned to Charles Holte Bracebridge and his wife, who lived in the Atherstone Hall mansion and, it is probable, chose to rent Aston Hall out. James Shaw, a relative of Morgan, resided there for a short time, but it appears that the house was empty in 1851.

An additional factor that may have contributed to the newlyweds staying at this special place could be the intercession of the famous writer Washington Irving who, as already mentioned, had a close relationship with the Osborne and Böhl de Faber families. In fact, María Manuela was born in 1827, coinciding with Irving's first visit to Spain. It is therefore possible that she was born exactly when he was finalising his *Tales of the Alhambra* in *El Cerrillo*. In any case, this was not an episodic relationship and, despite the distance, the author maintained close ties with Maria Manuela's family for years.

On the other hand, Irving had family in the area near Birmingham (at Edgbaston). His sister Sarah and her husband, who had two sons and two daughters, lived there. Irving had lived with them for several years, just before going to Spain. His brother-in-law was Henry Van Wart, an influential merchant and banker. During Irving's stay in Birmingham, the Van Warts, and Irving himself, visited Aston Hall several times (James Watt Jr still inhabited the house). Irving was so impressed with the building that it served as inspiration for his novel, *Bracebridge Hall* (actually, Bracebridge was the name of the last member of the Holte family lineage to live there). Thus, Irving was surely involved in arranging Maria Manuela's stay there for her honeymoon; moreover, we cannot reject the possibility of his nephew (who was a wine merchant) George Van Wart's involvement either.

Apparently, the stay at Birmingham left its mark on the young couple and led to them building relationships that they would maintain over the years. There is also no doubt that there was contact between Maria Manuela and the local members of the Catholic Church. Despite the circumstances of her marriage, she was a devout Catholic (one need only examine the history of her ancestors and descendants to prove this) and, being a follower of its precepts, she would necessarily have attended one of the Catholic churches in the city.

The situation in Birmingham and, in general, in England, wasn't exactly favourable to Catholics in early 1851. Towards the end of 1850, Pope Pius IX restored the Catholic hierarchy in the country, creating a structure of dioceses and parishes. This was the so-called "Papal aggression". Until then, there had been social discrimination against Catholics, who had even been deprived of their civil rights; indeed, this religious choice was interpreted from a political standpoint. British society viewed the Pope as the leader of a foreign state, so being Catholic meant giving up being a good English person, and having another regent and nation placed ahead of the Queen and the British Empire.

For example, William Ewart Gladstone, a former Prime Minister, published *The Vatican Decrees in Their Bearing on Civil Allegiance: A Political Expostulation*, wherein he stated: "No one can become convert [to Catholicism] without renouncing his moral and mental freedom, and placing his civil loyalty and duty at the mercy of another"[5]. In other words, Catholics could not be loyal subjects of the British Crown and the Pope at the same time.

The situation was in practice a matter of marginalisation, evident in many situations. For example, the number of Catholics living in Birmingham at the

---

5. William Ewart Gladstone, *The Vatican Decrees in their bearing on Civil Allegiance: A Political Expostulation*, Harper & Brothers, London, 1875, p. 13.

time wasn't negligible (there was a large Irish Catholic community) while, in 1848, there were only seven priests in the city and seventy in the whole diocese. Regarding the Catholic churches, there were only five (counting the cathedral and the Catholic cemetery's chapel) and a similar number of convents.

The fact of the matter is that the official announcement of the restoration of the Catholic Church's hierarchy in England caused a stir throughout the country, which swept right down from the Queen to the humblest of the social classes. The issue was even taken to parliament, where some members tried to pass a law to punish those who criminally assumed Catholic titles in England. At the same time, anti-papal demonstrations were taking place, like the meeting in Birmingham's Town Hall, on December 11th 1850, where about 8,000 people rallied.

Residing in Aston Hall, María Manuela most likely attended the Cathedral of St Chad, which was relatively close by. It is also likely that she had ties with a newly formed Community of Oratorians (followers of St Philip Neri), which had just been established in the city, in Alcester Street[6], near the cathedral, just a few blocks from where the Van Warts lived. They were led by a distinguished and prestigious scholar, a newly ordained Catholic priest by the name of John Henry Newman. Not long before, he had left an important position within the Anglican Church. His brilliant writings and speeches, full of the very best rhetoric, were useful elements for smoothing over the controversy that this sparked.

---

6. Shortly afterwards, they moved to their definitive address at Hagley Road.

Early Years

The Morgan-Osborne Family

Upon returning from their honeymoon, the newlyweds and, in general, the entire family, began an intense period of changes. Over a brief timespan, María Manuela's sisters married and the family patriarch, Thomas Osborne-Mann, died soon after, in 1854.

Cecilia married García de Porres y Castillo, the seventh Marquis of Castilleja del Campo, while Francisca Xaviera, who was called Paca by everyone in the family, married Antonio Rueda y Quintanilla, who was the eighth Marquis of Saltillo. Eventually, María Manuela Osborne and Francis Morgan's marriage was accepted by the whole family. Cecilia Böhl de Faber, who serves us again as witness, described it in one of his letters to Hartzenbusch, in April 1852:

> María Manuela lives happily and has fulfilled her Anglophile desires. Everything goes very well [...] because the husband is a good man and they are very fortunate in their union.[1]

The three sisters began to have children, and soon a new generation emerged. On March 12th 1852, Cecilia Böhl de Faber stated to her correspondent:

> Cecilia has given birth to a beautiful child. María Manuela had another boy, somewhat thin, but he is going to gain weight, given that he eats a lot.[2]

This situation extended over time and Cecilia Böhl de Faber wrote in the late fifties:

> Aurora remains well, surrounded by grandchildren, because my nieces do not want the world to end. How many children! Oh my God! María Manuela has three robust sons on Earth and one in Heaven, Cecilia four beautiful little ones, and Paca, the more cautious, has two children.[3]

However, the joys of birth were balanced out by a remarkable number of deaths, typical at that time among newborns. One of María Manuela's

---
1. Theodor Heinerman, *Cecilia Böhl de Faber y Juan Eugenio Hartzenbusch, una correspondencia inédita*. Espasa Calpe, Madrid, 1944, p. 134. (Translated by the author of this work).
2. Op. cit., p. 128.
3. Op. cit., p. 182.

sons did not survive childbirth and, in fact, may have been stillborn; his name is unknown, and he doesn't even appear in the family records. Aside from this, María Manuela bore four children: three boys and one girl. The eldest was Tomás, born in March 1852, followed by Augusto, in August 1853, Francisco Javier (the subject of this study) on January 18th 1857, and finally, Isabel, who arrived into the world in 1858.[4]

In particular, Francisco Javier's birth (Fr. Francis Morgan) was also reported by Cecilia Böhl de Faber in another of her letters:

> María Manuela gave birth to another child, named Francisco, like his father, and mother and child are well.[5]

The latter half of the 1850s, between the death of Thomas Osborne-Mann and the coming of age of his sons, was particularly fruitful for the Morgan-Osborne family. In the social field, María Manuela's position, as Osborne-Mann's eldest daughter, was increased by her husband Francis' position. He was a wine trade expert and partner in the business, who was asked to run the firm until the coming of age of his young brothers-in-law, Tomás and Juan Nicolás (Juanito, to the family), becoming their protector during this time.[6]

He had to combine this task with the management of his own business. In fact, of the nearly forty thousand *arrobas*[7] of spirits exported in 1858 from Port St Mary, five thousand belonged to (at the time, still named) Duff-Gordon and about fifteen hundred to the Morgan firm.[8]

In the course of their marriage, the Morgan-Osbornes acquired several properties in Port St Mary. First, in 1855, they purchased a large dwelling at 124 Larga Street (or Virgen de los Milagros Street) which included cellars, stables, etc. for María Manuela's sister, Cecilia Osborne, Marquise of Castilleja del Campo. The house consisted of a ground floor with nine rooms and a garden, a first floor with twelve rooms, and a second floor with a veranda. Its total surface area was 1,334 square meters. Later, in the summer of 1859, the Morgans acquired an adjacent house on Larga Street, facing Nevería Street (sometimes called *Castelar*), which enabled them to connect both buildings.

Between 1857 and 1858, they also acquired estates outside of town: first, a property near *El Cerrillo*, which was the Osbornes' family estate (probably

---

4. They had (and used in a suitable context) English versions of their names. These are: Thomas, Augustus, Francis Xavier and Elisabeth.
5. Diego de Valencina, *Cartas de Fernán Caballero*, Librería de los Sucesores de Hernando, Madrid, 1919, p. 202. (Translated by the author of this work).
6. A curious coincidence in relation to what would happen to Fr. Francis with the Tolkien brothers many years later.
7. A historical Spanish volumetric unit used to measure liquids, equivalent to 16.133 litres.
8. *Boletín oficial del Ministerio de Fomento*, Volumen 26, 1858, p. 573.

a piece of land with a house separated from it), and then a nearby farm. Although the houses belonged to the family for years (in fact, until the death of Augusto, the last member residing in Spain), it isn't clear if these estates were kept in the family after the death of Francis Morgan senior.

Their life, between the city and the countryside, ran as one would expect of members of the gentry, with a busy social life. In fact, visitors were common, although it seems that María Manuela had some problems:

> Catalina[9] is now staying at María Manuela, who is a great friend, and where she should remain, because they have a large mansion with no guests, even though Maria Manuela argues that Catalina annoys her husband.[10]

At other times, the guests were much more illustrious, such as the Duke of Montpensier[11], and Infant of Spain, who visited Port St Mary in 1858, and for whom María Manuela acted as proud host. Her aunt commented on this and wryly noted:

> María Manuela wrote me a long letter just to tell me in detail the accommodation they gave to the Infant.[12]

Regarding Francis Morgan, he adapted his life according to Spanish habits. A direct testimony of this comes from George John Cayley, a young man from a prominent Yorkshire family, who visited Spain for health reasons during the last months of 1851. As a result of this trip, he published a book titled *Las Alforjas, or Bridle Roads of Spain* in 1853, where he described his adventures.

Indeed, there is a chapter dedicated to the area of Cadiz. Cayley's companion in Port St Mary was Francis Morgan, then newly married and expecting his first child. The description of their meeting is illustrative of

---

9. Catalina des Fontaines y Barron was born in Cadiz in 1818. About the same age as María Manuela, her uncle William (Guillermo) Lonergan was one of the first partners of Thomas Osborne-Mann. His uncle Eustace (Eustaquio Servando Rafael) and his cousin William (Guillermo), son of the former, amassed a fortune in Mexico, where they established links that will be discussed later.
10. Op. cit. [5], p. 197.
11. Antoine Marie Philippe Louis d'Orleans, Duke of Montpensier (1824 - 1890) son of Louis Philippe III of France and member of the Spanish royal family by his marriage to María Luisa Fernanda of Borbon (daughter of King Fernando VII and sister of Queen Isabel II). As a result of the 1848 revolution, he had to leave France and went to England with his family (where they settled in Twickenham). Later, with his wife and children, he moved to Spain and settled in Seville, but they liked to visit the nearby cities of Cadiz, Port St Mary and Sanlucar de Barrameda. In 1868, he conspired in favor of the uprising that toppled his sister-in-law, Isabel II and even he aspired to (and almost obtained) the throne of Spain. After six years of a Republican regime, the throne passed to his nephew Alfonso XII (who married his daughter, María de las Mercedes). Montpensier became close friends with Cecilia Böhl de Faber.
12. Manuel Ravina Martín, *Cartas familiares inéditas de Fernán Caballero*, p. 208, in Milagros Fernández Poza y Mercedes García Pazos, (eds.), *Actas del encuentro Fernán Caballero, hoy*, Biblioteca de Temas Portuenses, Ayto. El Puerto de Santa María, El Puerto de Santa María, 1996. (Translated by the author of this work).

how Francis had adopted Spanish ways:

> I steamed across the blue bay, and breakfasted with Don Francisco[13] Morgan, a wine-merchant of Puerto de Santa Maria[14], to whom I had a letter. According to the custom of the country, there was wine on the table and, after breakfast, I drank a glass of sherry that was better than any I remember tasting before. Happening to say so, he said, "Do you like it? Very few Englishmen do at first. It is pure wine."
> "What?" said I. "Do you adulterate your wines, and own it without contrition?"
> "Without the slightest, for the mixture increases the cost of the wine. The natural dry wine which grows about Xeres is seldom sent to England unless specially ordered. It is flavoured, to suit the market, with a luscious sweet wine of the same neighbourhood, and tinted with what is called burnt wine; that is, wine boiled down till it is thick and dark-coloured. This creates a confusion of flavour, and destroys the fine clear twang of a natural vintage. We ourselves much prefer it unmixed, finding it much more wholesomer, as well as more palatable. If our English customers would learn to like sherry in its simple state, it would save us a good deal of trouble and expense."
> He took me to a large *bodega*[15] (cellar), and made me taste a few dozen pipes, of different ages; also the sweet sherry and burnt wine, neither of which were bad themselves, though I don't think they improved the original sherry.
> The Señora Morgan had a sister married to a *marques*[16] in Seville, and to him Don Francisco gave me a letter of introduction. He also gave me a letter of credit on a banker in Cadiz.[17]

As mentioned, from 1854, Morgan was the head of the business and, somehow, head of the Osborne household (in fact, he was the eldest man in the family), which also led to him dealing with several unpleasant tasks. For example, he had to deal with the repercussions of the suicide of Cecilia Böhl de Faber's third husband, Antonio Arrom, during Easter 1859. It was a shock for the whole family, given the circumstances of the death.[18]

Indirectly, we know the role of Francis Morgan in the matter. It was he who received the tragic news and had to inform his mother-in-law, Aurora.

---

13. In Spanish in the original.
14. Ibid.
15. Ibid.
16. Ibid.
17. George John Cayley, *Las Alforjas, or the Bridle Roads of Spain*, Bradbury and Evans / Richard Bentley, London, 1853, pp. 64-65.
18. Antonio Arrom, the third husband of Cecilia Böhl de Faber, was unsuccessful in any of the enterprises he undertook. Finally, he achieved, thanks to the influence of his wife's family, to be Spanish Consul in Australia, which he tried to reconcile with the development of various businesses. When everything seemed to improve, his partner betrayed him, pushing him to ruin. The desperation drove him to commit suicide in London, where he was when he discovered his partner's scam. According to one of the biographers of Cecilia Böhl de Faber, he shot himself in the head in Blenheim Park, which was owned by the Duke of Marlborough. Arrom carried with him a suicide note, expressing his desire for his body

This is referred to in a letter that the Marquis of Villarreal and Purullena wrote to his brother, Fermín Iribarren (who was married to Cecilia's sister, Ángela, and was therefore the deceased man's brother-in-law):

> Holy Wednesday, Morgan received notice by telegraph of Arrom's death in London, with the aggravating circumstance, for himself and the family, of it being suicide. He waited for a while to communicate this unfortunate event to Aurora, and finally it seems that he did so on Friday. Aurora wrote to Cecilia [...] I think, telling the bad news.[19]

It seems that María Manuela, albeit with less intensity than her sisters and brothers-in-law, also took part in the infamous bad treatment of Cecilia Böhl de Faber after her third marriage, which resulted in the couple being forced to leave Port St Mary shortly after their wedding. This affront was finally repaired, not without some lingering resentment, after Antonio Arrom's suicide. From this moment, her nieces tried to ingratiate her, carrying out several charitable actions:

> When I got here I found my house stocked with everything: sugar, ham, butter, chocolate, chickpeas, coffee, tea, etc. Imagine who was the fairy. The idea came from Candelaria; my nieces did not want to fall behind. Cecilia magically put a barrel of olive oil in the basement. María Manuela filled the coal bunker. What high price for so many courtesies received! It does not mean that I am not grateful.[20]

The new decade began shortly after the suicide and saw major changes: Tomás Osborne, the eldest of the Thomas Osborne-Mann's sons, reached his coming of age and took control of the business after finishing his studies in England.

Delving deeper into the figure of Tomás Osborne Böhl de Faber, we know that he was a wealthy heir, and physically graceful, as indicated by the portraits of the time. On April 1860, Tomás got married to Enriqueta Guezala Power, daughter of a prominent military man of Canarian roots, in Seville. They had ten children, six sons and four daughters. The eldest son was born in 1861 and was named Tomás, following the family tradition. Among the other children were Roberto and Antonio. Roberto was an entrepreneur with great business instincts, much like his grandfather. He left the wine business and moved to Seville, where he founded one of the best known beer houses in Spain: *La Cruz del Campo*, which is known today as *Cruzcampo*. Antonio, a Jesuit priest, was a promoter of the Astronomical

---

to be buried in the place of his death, with a cross erected over his grave.
19. Op. cit. [12], p. 195.
20. Op. cit. [5], p. 182.

Observatory of Cartuja, in Granada.

On the other hand, Juan Nicolás Osborne Böhl de Faber, María Manuela's youngest brother (she was, in fact, his godmother), joined the Diplomatic Service and didn't marry. His life was spent primarily in Italy, France and Russia. He earned the title of Count of Osborne from Pope Pius IX in 1869, which was inherited by his nephew, Tomás Osborne Guezala, who was his brother's oldest son.

The new generation of Osbornes, led by Tomás Osborne Böhl de Faber, took control of the family business (the purely Osborne side of the business, that is) shortly after, and the Morgan-Osborne family moved to London. It was not at all a matter of rivalry, since the relationship with Tomás Osborne had always been good - in fact, Francis Morgan shared many hobbies with him. For instance, they went hunting at *Coto Doñana* together on several occasions.[21] Rather, it was to do with a change of environment after the long period spent in Spain; the move also coincided with their children beginning their studies in England.

The Morgan family, as with the Osbornes, cultivated an extended network of social relations. Proof of this is the list of subscribers for the book that Aaron Augustus Morgan published in 1856 (a translation of *Ecclesiastes*), which was financed by the contributions of more than two hundred people, who were most likely doing so more out of friendship than any real interest in the work.

It seems clear that this was primarily a list of Morgan family acquaintances (which includes the "Spanish branch" as well as its members who ran the business in London), though there were also some members of the Anglican Church, which the author himself belonged to, and scholars of biblical themes. Among the subscribers are several residents from Spain, such as Tomás Osborne and his brother Juan Nicolás, as well as Daniel Macpherson, a former partner from Duff-Gordon. There are other noteworthy groups to be found too. For example, there are several London wine importers, like David Hart, John Blackeway, and the retired Charles Dixon; so too several residents of Dulwich (where the family patriarch, Aaron Morgan, settled), and also noblemen: the Duke of Norfolk, Lord Bridport, Baroness Mallet, Lord Byron (cousin to the famous author), etc.

It is also interesting to note the Morgans' (through Maria Morgan's marriage to Captain Morgan Sykes) and the Osbornes' (because of their relationship with Lord Shore, the father-in-law of Thomas Osborne-Mann's brother) links with the East India Company. Several prominent members of this company are listed, such as Colonel Sykes, Captain Sturt and, among others, Sir Frederick Currie. Additionally, there are names associated with

---

21. The Coto Doñana is now a National Park situated in Andalusia, just south-west of Seville. It is one of Europe's most valuable wetlands and a major site for migrating birds.

Birmingham, members of the Shaw family (relatives of the Morgans), Charles Holte Bracebridge, related to Aston Hall, as we saw, and Henry Van Wart, Washington Irving's brother-in-law.

The truth is that various circumstances distinguished the Morgan-Osbornes from the rest of the family and pointed them out as the most British of all the Osbornes. Without denying their integration into Spanish life, while other family members abandoned their English roots in a heartbeat[22], they played with this duality at their convenience in many cases, an approach that was probably favoured due to having close family in the United Kingdom (in the Morgan branch).

In hindsight, this attitude, as evidenced in María Manuela's wedding in England, and in her husband's refusal to convert to Catholicism, which would have been very useful for him, was repeated in subsequent actions by other family members. For example, a good illustrative case is demonstrated by the second of their sons, Augustus Morgan, who had two wills. Having lived much of his life in Port St Mary (he was born and died there), as one of its best-known citizens, it said this in his English will[23]:

> I declare that I am a British Citizen and that I have never lost my English domicile[24] and I have no intention of doing so notwithstanding that I have for some years resided in Spain, and propose to continue to do so, such residence being for my own convenience and health and not intended in any way to interfere with or alter my British Citizenship.[25]

The Morgan-Osbornes lived in England from 1869 until 1876. The family home was located in London, at 138 Harley Street, very close to Regents Park. However, in the census of 1871, only two of the children (Tomás and Isabel) were residing there, since Augusto and the future Father, Francis, were away at school. It may be surprising that his brother Tomás was not with them, but alas he was born with a disability and could never have led a normal life, in education or work, as he could never have properly performed any task in the wine trading business.

Residing in London, instead of in Spain, undoubtedly made it easier to visit their children, as well as their nephew Tomás Osborne Guezala (the eldest son of Tomás Osborne Böhl de Faber), who began his studies at Baylis House, Slough, in 1872, and who afterwards went to Beaumont College[26], a Jesuit boarding school. However, the choice of location of their

---

22. This is especially noticeable in María Manuela's sisters, so it is unimaginable, for instance, that she gave her name to a livestock of fighting Bulls, as her sister Paca, Marquise of Saltillo did.
23. Actually, he had two wills, one in Spain and one in England.
24. Although he lived in London for several years in the late 19th century (at 12 Aldford Street, Park Lane), his "English domicile" was, for a long time, a room at the Rembrandt Hotel in London.
25. Osborne Archives.
26. Bernardo Rodríguez Caparrini, *Alumnos españoles en el internado jesuita de Beaumont (Old*

home in London did not seem to be a casual one. Very close to Harley Street is St James', Spanish place, for a long time a church of reference for British Catholics, with a strong Spanish connection. In María Manuela's obituary, the famous Catholic newspaper, *The Tablet*, it notes her as a parishioner of this church and indicates her relationship with the nuns of the Convent of Marie Reparatrice, which was also near their home. It is, therefore, no coincidence that her daughter Isabel, a probable companion and collaborator in her actions in support of the congregation, took the habits of this religious order.

However, their time in England was cut short by the untimely death of Francis Morgan on January 31st 1876, when he was fifty-five and his young children had not yet come of age. From this moment on, his sons and daughter, firstly because of their education and then because of the occupations they chose, were dispersed and none of them married or had children (the two eldest died unmarried; Isabel, as mentioned, became a nun, and Francisco Javier, who would of course become Fr. Francis, a Catholic priest). These events eventually led to the extinction of the family line.

Cecilia Böhl de Faber, who once again witnessed the impact of events on the family, described what happened in a letter to the secretary of the Duke of Montpensier, Antonio de Latour:

> We mourn the death of Morgan, who was consumed by laryngitis, husband to my niece María Manuela; it happened in London.[27]

María Manuela frequently travelled, following her husband's death, and she included a clause in her will stating that she wanted to be buried in the nearest Catholic cemetery to wherever her death occurred. Eventually, she died in Port St Mary.

Without seeking to anticipate what follows, it's good to look back for a moment, in order to complete the family portrait, paying special attention to the only preserved picture of the whole family, which can be dated to 1865, at Port St Mary. The photo shows a well-to-do family. The father, Francis Morgan, is looking at the camera with a serious expression, accentuated by his long sideburns. The mother, María Manuela, with a hint of a smile, is wearing an elegant dark dress. The couple's daughter, Isabel, who is fair-haired, unlike her mother, sits smiling between them. Behind, standing, are the three sons. Francisco Javier, with an air of shyness, is not yet old enough to wear a suit; next to him are Tomás, the eldest son, dressed in a white suit, and the round-faced Augusto, wearing a dark suit and a bowler hat.

Windsor, Inglaterra) 1874-1880, Miscelánea Comillas: Revista de Ciencias Humanas y Sociales, p. 246.
27. Santiago Montoto, (Ed.), *Cartas inéditas de Fernán Caballero*, S. Aguirre Torre, 1961, p 18. (Translated by the author of this work).

Francisco Javier (Francis Xavier in the anglicised version) was named after his aunt, Paca (Francisca Xaviera), and his great-grandmother. He was usually called Curro by his family, being the Andalusian colloquial version of Francis, and sometimes, when speaking in English, they also called him Frank. He spent his early childhood in Port St Mary with his brothers and cousins, in particular with his uncle Tomás' children. However, in the years that followed, his life would take him to England, where he would spend the best part of the rest of his life.

Education in England

The term "public school" is generally only used within the English-speaking world. Interestingly, there is a contradiction between the origin of the concept and the model of education which eventually emerged from it. In the early 19th century, when this terminology came into use, it referred to schools open to all people, that could also charge a fee for attendance. By the middle of the century, the definition of "public school" changed to refer to *elite* schools, places which offered a higher level of education and targeted the upper classes, by way of exorbitant fees.

Examining the most prominent English public schools of that time (in other words, reviewing the best educational offerings of the United Kingdom), we see a list that includes the most traditional and well-known schools: Eton, Harrow and Westminster. The other six on this list should also be mentioned: Winchester, Charterhouse, Rugby, Shrewsbury, St Paul, and Merchant Taylors.

None of them was a possible destination for young Catholics; on the contrary, a mutual exclusion existed between them. Since they were not welcome in these establishments, Catholics did not want their children socialising with Anglicans (or members of other religious faiths). To be sure, Catholic status in English society was complicated, almost marginal in many matters, and education was no exception.

Until 1791, Catholic schools were not allowed in England and, even after that, laws denied many civil rights to Roman Catholics until 1829. Education was a particularly thorny issue when you take into account that the impossibility of gaining entry to the best schools (and universities) prevented access to the highest social positions, political responsibilities, and the top intellectual circles.

Almost all prestigious Catholic schools' founders came from the mainland, particularly religious figures who had taken refuge in the United Kingdom due to the French Revolution or the Napoleonic wars. Thus, in 1794, Jesuits from Liege opened Stonyhurst, while Benedictine exiles established Ampleforth in 1806 and Downside in 1813.

In addition to these schools, there were also the seminaries of Oscott and Shaw, where young people who had no intention of being ordained could also be educated. In fact, their fees covered the study costs for those who had decided to be priests. In many cases, these aspiring priests helped the youngest of the students with educational tasks, acting as counsellors, tutors, etc.

The systems used within Catholic schools were completely different from public school methods. Their fundamentals and principles were drawn chiefly from the mainland, which often conflicted with British traditions and idiosyncrasies; moreover, Catholic schools had an educational level significantly lower than what was offered by their public counterparts. Until the mid-nineteenth century, there was a certain complacency among Catholics about this, but various circumstances would soon cause them to become openly concerned.

To understand the intricacy of this issue, it is necessary to reconstruct the different types of Catholics living in England at that time. By 1850, they did not exceed 3.5% of the population and, far from being a homogeneous group, three main branches could be distinguished.

On the one hand, there were those who had remained attached to their faith throughout the centuries, against the dominant Protestantism, despite the persecution and marginalisation they had endured. It was a group that practiced a static form of Catholicism, stuck in the past and lacking in intellectual brilliance, whose followers lived especially in rural areas. Only a small amount of them belonged to the upper classes, and they were mostly traders or craftsmen.

Alongside these "Old Catholics" coexisted an emerging group of Anglican converts, many of whom belonged to the upper classes, who were accepted with some reluctance by traditional Catholics. In this context, it is of particular importance to note the so-called Oxford Movement, a thinking process born within the Church of England, which criticised its spiritual stagnation, its doctrinal unorthodoxy and the interference of the state in matters of faith. This movement would be the starting point for the conversion of a select group of people to Catholicism, many of whom had been educated at Oxford or Cambridge. Arguably, these conversions not only introduced new minds to Catholicism, but they also brought in people who had been instructed in the finest British educational traditions.

The third branch was formed of the many Irish immigrants, devout Catholics who usually belonged to the lowest social classes. As a result of the industrial revolution, many Irish came to work in English cities and made up the largest group of Catholics in England.

The advent of converts as an emerging group, despite this group's comparatively small size, marked the beginning of a revolution within the Catholic Church in England, which coincided with other events, such as the restoration of the Catholic hierarchy. The pressure exerted by this new group, whose members were economically and socially privileged, became evident in the education of their children. They wanted a Catholic education equal to that received by non-Catholics, or a similar one to what they themselves had enjoyed in their childhood, and petitioned for the creation of a Catholic public school. To accomplish this, the most important step was to find a prominent Catholic scholar willing to become the promoter of this project, something which would most likely compromise said individual's prestigious standing. Naturally, few people came forth.

Catholics had been excluded from superior education for centuries. In 1829, when they were finally allowed to attend universities, the Catholic hierarchy, in a curiously narrow minded gesture, issued a warning against traditional English universities like Oxford or Cambridge, and imposed a ban on non-Catholic colleges and schools, which was not reversed until 1895. Under these conditions, the great Catholic minds had either studied abroad or were converts who had enjoyed a good education at Oxford or Cambridge before their conversion.

It was John Henry Newman, probably the most notable convert of 19th century England, who accepted the challenge and undertook this project to gain an improved Catholic educational establishment. Newman created a Catholic public school (albeit with some peculiarities, such as headquarters in the city rather than in the country) within the Birmingham Oratory. He himself had established the oratory years before the creation of this school.

The role of a group of prominent Catholics, who were mostly converts from the Oxford Movement, was essential in the establishment of the Oratory School. Among them were Edward Bellasis and James Hope-Scott, who were co-founders. Both of them were lawyers and held important political positions. They sent their children to the new school, with Richard Bellasis, eldest son of Edward Bellasis, being the first pupil to enrol. More Catholics, particularly converts, supported the initiative. However, it was the backing of the Duke of Norfolk (an old Catholic and one of the most influential men in the United Kingdom), who sent his children to the new school, which largely helped to overcome some initial reluctance among the people.

The Birmingham Oratory School was opened on May 1st 1859. It was the first school that offered both a sense of British, thanks to its public school model, and Catholic ideologies. However, it did not have the easiest of beginnings. One of the first obstacles to overcome was Newman himself being largely rejected among Catholics both old and new.

As Newman's biography attests to, he was as rich in his passions and yearnings as he was in his intellectual curiosity. By the time the school was established in 1859, his life had already been punctuated by several remarkable events. He was born in 1801 to a heavily religious Anglican family and, after studying at Oxford[1], Newman was ordained as an Anglican

---

[1]. At this time, he befriended Blanco White, a friend of Frasquita Larrea, from Spain. He would go on to follow a path opposite to that of Newman: from Catholicism to Anglicanism.

priest, driven by a profound religious vocation. After distinguishing himself as a scholar, he was appointed vicar of Saint Mary's, the church of the University of Oxford. It provided a platform for the dissemination of the principal ideas of the Oxford Movement, since he was one of its leaders, along with John Keble, Richard Hurrell Froude and Edward Pusey.

However, his ideas distanced him from Anglicanism and, after a period of spiritual retirement, he decided to convert to Catholicism and was subsequently ordained a Roman Catholic priest. Newman set out for Italy and, on his return in 1848, founded the first English Oratory in Birmingham, a congregation of priests in the style of the Community founded by Saint Philip Neri in the 16th century. After a brief hiatus — Newman was invited to become the founder and first rector of a new university that had been established in Ireland for Catholics — he returned permanently to Birmingham, where he became tied to the Oratory and its school for the rest of his life.

In this new task, he had to overcome several obstacles. On a personal level, many accused him of being too liberal, and even his fidelity to the Catholic cause was questioned, as was his conversion. Newman converted to Roman Catholicism during one of the most conservative historical moments in the history of the Catholic Church, and this had an effect on him and his works, such as the founding of the Oratory School.

Not all of his problems arose from outside. In his leadership role, he had to take decisive action shortly after the establishment of the school, on account of a dispute between two of the staff members. The organisational approach conceived by Newman involved a two-headed administration supervised by him. On the one hand, the academic aspects were to be managed by the Father Prefect, a head teacher responsible for educational issues as well as matters of discipline. At the same time, Newman established a Dame system; that is, an independent structure of houses managed by reputable ladies, separated from educational issues, responsible for the accommodation and care of the school's students.

The first Father Prefect, Nicholas Darnell, an Oratorian with a wealth of educational experience, had a conflict of interest with Frances Wootten, the head of the ladies. This revealed how Darnell had his own ideas about the school, which were quite different from the concepts of his leader. Newman resolved this crisis in two ways: by replacing Darnell with Fr. Ambrose St John (a close friend of Newman since his conversion), and by modifying his own role in order to participate more actively in the school's daily life, even performing teaching duties.

Newman enjoyed running the school, despite the problems faced at the start and in the course of maintaining the project, and students who attended his classes received lessons and advice from a truly passionate individual.

He was called simply "Father" by them; clearly he was an important point of reference for them, both in their spiritual and personal spheres. Rather than maintaining a distance from his charges, Newman cherished their friendship and even shared insights into his own tastes, including his admiration for the novels of Walter Scott.

Until he reached old age, Newman monitored all students monthly, testing them orally on the work they had done during the previous month. He also encouraged the highest levels of honesty from the boys, with no room given for pettiness or unpleasantness. In addition, at the end of every term, he spoke with each of them about their progress and behavior.

The basic educational concept of the Oratory School was of a "liberal education". The objective was not only to obtain the immediate benefits of factual knowledge, but also to cultivate minds with the ultimate goal of pursuing the perfection of the intellect. Newman used the study of the classics as his main instrument, but he also went a step further, developing a broader curriculum to that of public schools, including modern languages and mathematics, while the boys were encouraged to read stimulating books.

The fact of the matter is that, mainly thanks to the talent and dedication of Newman, the school quickly progressed. He spoke about it in a letter after its third year of activity:

> When we began it was a simple experiment, and lookers-on seemed to be surprised when they found we had in half a year a dozen; but at the end of our third year we now have seventy. [...] are seriously alarmed at the responsibilities which we have brought on ourselves. As all other schools are increasing in number, it is a pleasant proof of the extension of Catholic education.[2]

In 1868, nine years after the founding of the Oratory School, the project seemed to have consolidated. The number of students approached seventy, and the annual rate per pupil was around one hundred pounds. St John and Frances Wootten continued in their tasks, though both were beginning to suffer health problems, which would prove to be fatal some years later.[3]

Newman continued his tireless, careful management of school affairs by personally checking its accounts and also monitoring the academic development of each student (which included the onerous task of writing letters to their parents). Moreover, he was often involved in extra activities, such as collaborating on the adaptation and direction of "Latin plays" for school festivals, or helping the older students to prepare their applications for other centres (in particular, the University of London).

---

2. Wilfrid Meynell, *Cardinal Newman*, Burns and Oates, London, 1907. p. 83.
3. Due to health problems, Ambrose St John left his position in 1872 and Mrs. Wootten followed suit in 1875. Both would die soon after (he in 1875 and she in 1876).

In 1868, a young Francis Xavier Morgan, who was eleven at the time, arrived at the Oratory School. His educational cycle there lasted six years, until 1874. It is interesting to note that these years coincide with a particularly complicated time in Spanish history: the so-called *Sexenio Revolucionario*.[4] During this period, sherry merchants benefitted from several political decisions that saw a reduction in customs duties, aimed at establishing a free trade economy, and an increase of exports to record high levels. However, the new and unstable political regime wasn't welcomed by many, including the Morgan-Osborne family, who were supporters of a traditional Spain.

Francis Morgan[5] wasn't the only member of his family at the school. A few years before his own admission, in 1865, his older brother Augusto began his studies at the Oratory. They remained there together until 1872, when Augusto completed his schooling.

It should be noted that this choice of school wasn't at all arbitrary. Instead, the Morgans' social standing led to them searching for an educational institution of the highest level. The requirement for it to be Catholic meant that the options were certainly restricted, even though, in the mid-sixties of the 19th century, Catholics had a wider choice than even twenty years before then.

Among the new Catholic schools, it is worth mentioning Beaumont College (also named St Stanislaus College), which was founded just two years after the Oratory School, in Old Windsor, Berkshire (Eton was only a few miles away, on the other side of the Thames).

Beaumont was a Jesuit boarding school but, unlike similar Jesuit establishments such as Stonyhurst, the oldest of this congregation in England, its methods were different. They diverged from the mainland systems and, over time, its changes and developments were imitated by many other schools. Moreover, Beaumont College was chosen as the educational institution for most of the families who were contemporary to the Morgans; not only the Osbornes from Spain, but also the Galtons, Roman Catholic cousins from England.

Despite the existence of Beaumont, the Morgans decided to enrol their

---

4. *Sexenio revolucionario* (the six-year revolution). In September 1868, a military uprising overthrew the Spanish queen Isabel II and sought to establish a democratic monarchy. Unfortunately, historical circumstances, such as problems arising from the Carlist wars, the colonial conflicts, and the economic crisis, prevented its viability. The initial idea was to restore the monarchy with a king who would obey the democratic system. Once the Borbons were eliminated (Alfonso, son of Isabel II, and the Duke of Montpensier) the honour fell to Amedeo of Savoy, Duke of Aosta. However, he was unable to cope with the complex situation caused by the problems noted above and soon abdicated. This led to the establishment of the First Spanish Republic, but a few months later, in December 1874, the Borbon monarchy was restored through Alfonso XII, which marked the end of the attempted revolution.

5. From this point onward, when Francis Morgan is named, it refers to Francis Xavier (or Francisco Javier) Morgan Osborne, the future Fr. Francis Morgan and object of this work; his father, with whom he shared his name, will barely be mentioned.

sons at the Oratory School. This choice is especially significant as it shows that, even from Spain, the family maintained enough ties with England to know what was going on there. It also suggests that their honeymoon in Birmingham had been a determining factor.

Vocation

At the Oratory School, its religious formation had great importance, and its boys were called upon to be pillars of the English Roman Catholics amongst the privileged classes. Catholics were a small group at the time, constantly fighting against social marginalisation. This situation could only be remedied with a firm commitment to their beliefs, especially for those who enjoyed the highest social positions.

Hence, a strong emphasis was placed on knowing at least the basics of the religion, learning its prayers, and an in-depth study of the catechism, to the point where, every week, the students were reviewed in pairs under the personal supervision of either Newman or the Father Prefect. Additionally, the content of subjects such as English, Latin and Greek was directed so as to introduce the study of the Holy Scriptures.

During the academic period, individual events of the liturgical year were commemorated and the boys were involved in these celebrations. In particular, the *Via Crucis*[1] was revived every Friday during Lent, a procession on the school grounds was performed on *Corpus Christi*[2], accompanied by a band, and all students participated in a three-day retreat during Easter, where a priest unaffiliated with the Oratory was invited.

However, the school wasn't a seminary, and its primary objective wasn't to mould priests, but rather Catholic laypeople who would be engaged with their faith (although many future priests were former students of the school). There were several differences between the Oratory School and a seminary, but undoubtedly the fundamental divergence lay in the format and educational content. The Oratory School prioritised the teaching of the classics, as did most public schools, following a humanistic model in the manner of Oxford or Cambridge, while other Catholic schools and seminaries were mainly focused on the lives, major events, and writings of the Fathers of the Church.

On an ordinary day, while Morgan was a student here, the boys rose at half past six, said their prayers, and attended a seven o'clock Mass. Afterwards, they were at their first class until half past eight, when they ate

---

1. The Stations of the Cross (or, in Latin, *Via Crucis*) is a representation of the Passion of Christ carrying the cross to his crucifixion along several stations. It is often performed as a play, in a spirit of reparation for the sufferings that Jesus endured.
2. Religious festival in honour of the Eucharist. *Corpus Christi* is celebrated on the Thursday after the eighth Sunday of Easter (that is, sixty days after Easter Sunday).

breakfast. This lasted until half past nine, when they returned to classrooms until midday. At that time, they gathered for the *Angelus*[3] and then had lunch. Between half past two and five o'clock, they attended afternoon classes, followed by an hour of playtime. Tea time was at six, after which the boys had the opportunity to recite the Rosary, followed by an hour of quiet study before dinner. Once finished, they went to bed. In their bedrooms, before lights-out, they prayed together, while excerpts from spiritual classics were read out by one of the Fathers; they would then kneel for personal prayers, before finally going to sleep.

There were also non-religious extracurricular activities available. For example, the students were given a few hours for drawing and practising on musical instruments once a week. Sports, including competitions with other schools, were also widely practised. Following an innovative concept that emerged in the mid-nineteenth century, public schools gave great prominence to sports. As a result, the belief that they could inspire virtues, develop manhood, and build character, became very popular.

One of the most ambitious of these extracurricular activities was the preparation of theatrical plays in Latin, based on classic texts; these were usually from Plautus or Terence. In fact, *The Phormio* by Terence was one of the most popular and was performed on three different occasions between 1865 and 1872. The roles were played by the students and the cast included important future figures related to the Oratory and its school. It also featured prominent members of the city's public life since, despite their status as Catholics, all students belonged to the upper classes.[4]

In 1872, the two Morgan brothers, Francis and Augustus, were in the cast of one of these Latin plays. While Augusto's performance wasn't highlighted, Francis Morgan won much praise in the role of Sophrona, an old nurse. A book that was compiled for the history of those representations even indicates as much:

> We were favoured by Fr. Francis with the apparition of a veritable hag, went with such spirit and humour as I never remember before.[5]

Obviously it was a review made years later, after Morgan had already become a priest but, interestingly, this is the first time that his affable character and his inherent joy are alluded to. In fact, as we shall see, throughout his life his personality led to him being a victim of several misunderstandings,

---

3. The *Angelus* is a prayer dedicated to Mary and the Annunciation, repeated three times each day, at morning, noon and evening, although many people recite it only at noon.
4. Some of them as important as the second son of the Duke of Norfolk, Lord Edmund Talbot, who would be appointed Lord Lieutenant of Ireland.
5. Edward Bellasis, *The Phormio at the Oratory school, by an "old boy"*, Nichols and Sons, London, 1881, p.15.

because his behaviour contrasted with some of the more rigid British habits.

At any rate, Francis Morgan had the privilege (especially enjoyed by students in the early years of the Oratory) of priceless, direct and continuous contact with John Henry Newman. If anything stood out in the school at that time, it was Newman's constant presence. His virtues and qualities in the religious and intellectual fields did not go unnoticed among the young students. One of the greatest privileges for the boys was being selected to visit his study, in groups of five or six, and listen to him playing the violin.

However, not all was idyllic. Another student of Spanish origin, José María Gordon Prendergast, also from the area of Cadiz (born in Jerez de la Frontera a year before Francis Morgan), described in his memoirs how physical punishment was still employed in the school. This was inflicted by Fr. Ambrose St John who, unlike Newman, "was by no means thin or ascetic. He possessed a powerful arm.".[6]

It seems that Gordon was a difficult student who didn't speak fluent English when he arrived at the school and his attitude, as noted in his memoirs, was quite inappropriate. In any case, he remained at the school for only one year. He must also have been one of Fr. Ambrose St John's last victims as, after more than a decade as headmaster, he was replaced for health reasons in 1872 by Fr. John Norris (who years later would become Provost of the Community).

Although Morgan didn't excel at sport, or have an outstanding academic vocation, it seems that religious life appealed to him, probably because of Newman's influence. He was not the only boy who felt this attraction because, although the Oratory School wasn't a seminary, it undeniably became a breeding ground for future priests, many of whom would become members of the wider community when they reached adulthood.

Several of Morgan's classmates of a similar age would make up the core of the Oratory from the end of the 19th century until well into the 20th. The priests that emerged from the "Old School Boys", or former students of the Oratory School who had been in contact with Newman, are certainly a group that shaped and cemented the Community of the Birmingham Oratory, and were responsible for its development.

Among the Oratorians with whom Francis Morgan shared his life were the Bellasis brothers, Anthony Pollen, whose parents were influential figures who had converted to Catholicism as a result of the Oxford Movement, plus Francis Joseph Bacchus, who studied the life and works of Newman, the long-lived Irishman, Denis Sheil, Robert Eaton, choir director for many years, and Edward Pereira, a British subject whose family came from Portugal.

---

6. José María Gordon, *The Chronicles of a Gay Gordon*, Cassell and Company Limited, London, 1921, p.24.

After their last years at the Oratory, the students were required to start specific training for a chosen discipline, usually the army or further education, geared towards either a secular or a religious occupation. Francis Morgan began his studies in the middle of the 1870s. From the steps he took, and his subsequent actions, it was clear he already had intentions of joining the clergy.

He had to evaluate his limited alternatives. He could return to Spain, as his brother Augusto had, to join the family business, or live off its income. He could also continue his studies in Spain, where there were equally prestigious higher education institutions, some quite close to his home, such as the University of Seville. Finally, he had the option of going abroad, to Italy or Germany for example, to complete his education there. He definitely couldn't attend a traditional English University like Oxford, where ironically some of his ancestors[7], and even Newman, had attended, since Catholics were forbidden by Papal Decree from studying at Oxford or Cambridge.

However, Morgan chose a different alternative and enrolled in the Catholic University College, which was established in Kensington in 1874. It was an ambitious project, promoted by Cardinal Manning, the then head of the Catholic Church in England. Manning was the successor of Cardinal Wiseman (born in Seville and famous for his novel, *Fabiola*) and defended positions that were largely opposed to Newman's ideas.

The Catholic University hosted a very small group of young Catholics, most of whom were from the wealthy families who had contributed financially to its creation. Mgr Capel was appointed Rector, and was surrounded by a group of distinguished professors. However, the project was a failure, and many students, including Francis Morgan, remained for only a few months in Kensington. Apparently a loss of confidence in Capel, due to his financial mismanagement, and gossip about his personal life, led to the University's closure, although there were other underlying reasons. Surely the most compelling cause could be found in the opposition to his ideas of this university model, expressed by Jesuits, influential Catholic families, old Catholics, and converts, who preferred a Catholic higher education in an Oxford context.

After this brief experience at the Catholic University, Francis Morgan decided to continue his studies in a similar institution, though one now necessarily outside of England. The chosen country was Belgium, which

---

7. Since the early 17th century, there is knowledge of Francis Morgan's ancestors (by the Osborne branch) who studied in Oxford. The first was the Rev. Peter Osborne who attended Oriel College circa 1620. Most of his descendants studied at Exeter College (some as Daniel Osborne, born in 1669 and died in 1710, who is buried in the chapel of the College). The older brother of Thomas Osborne-Mann (the grandfather of Francis Morgan), that is, his great-uncle Rev. Peter Osborne (1776-1850) also studied at Exeter College. He was the last of the English Osbornes to do so because he died childless. Obviously none of them were Catholic.

was very close to the United Kingdom, at the prestigious Catholic University of Louvain.

Louvain was usually frequented by young British people who could find there what they were denied at home. Somehow, the ancient city and its centenary University reminded many of the classic English centres. It certainly stood up in comparisons to Oxford.

The Catholic University of Louvain is regarded as the oldest of its kind in the world, although there were periods during the 18th and early 19th centuries where it was closed. Following Belgian independence in 1830, the University was reopened by Belgian bishops and regained its notoriety. In fact, it reached high levels of prestige thanks to figures like Cardinal Mercier, who promoted a revival of Catholic philosophy.

During his adventure in Belgium, Morgan was accompanied by one of his English cousins from the Galton family, called Hubert.[8] Their stay in Louvain was short, lasting only a couple of years. Moreover, it was marked by the already mentioned death of Morgan's father, in January 1876.

After Louvain, Morgan returned to Birmingham. He decided to be ordained and was the third alumnus of the Oratory School to join its Community. The first were the Bellasis brothers, Richard and Louis, who were pioneers in everything related to the Oratory.

In his absence, the Oratory (and its school) suffered two major losses. In 1875, Fr. Ambrose St John, Newman's right hand and, for many years, Father Prefect, died. A few months later, Mrs Wooten, Dame of the Oratory School, and a leading figure in its first years, also passed away. These deaths, along with others, such as that of Fr. Edward Caswall (convert priest, well known for his translations and hymns), occurred shortly after Francis Morgan's return. This ushered in a gradual renewal of the Oratory, whose founding fathers were being replaced by a new generation.

Like all who aspired to join the Community, Morgan had to overcome the long period of being an Oratorian novitiate, which he began on September 18th 1877. Those years were necessarily demanding, under the supervision of Newman who, despite trying to be a devoted friend to his colleagues and subordinates, was also strict in his compliance with the rules, which sometimes caused confusion.[9]

---

8. Morgan had four cousins in the Catholic side of the Galton family, all of similar ages, called Hubert, Howard, Compton and Charles. Charles and Compton were priests (Compton became bishop), while Howard studied law at the University of London. Hubert decided on a military career and had a close friendship with Francis Morgan, especially in the latter part of his life. Compton and Charles received at least a part of their school education in Beaumont, where Charles would return years later as a teacher of Geography. Meanwhile, Howard and Hubert had done part of their studies at the Oratory School; Howard between 1868-1870, and Hubert during the academic year 1874-1875.

9. One example is what happened to Fr. Denis Sheil when he was a novice (many years later, he would become Provost of the Oratory). He told Newman that he felt sick and asked permission to spend a night at Rednal, the Community retreat in the country. Newman replied, "You know Denis, a novice is not

During his novitiate, Morgan bore witness to the single most central event in the history of the Birmingham Oratory when, in May 1879, John Henry Newman, the leader of the Community, was inducted as cardinal by Pope Leo XIII. This news was greeted with joy, and various celebrations took place upon Newman's return from Rome in July.

At the end of that month, the old cardinal received two tributes, the first in the context of the Oratory, and the second in relation to the school. On Sunday the 20th, after the Mass, the Oratory School Society (whose members were former pupils) gave him a set of High Mass vestments and a cope[10] of red cloth, richly embroidered with gold, according to his new status. During the ceremony, Lord Edmund Talbot read out a brief address (signed by members of this society, including the Morgan brothers), in which they praised Newman's personal influence and guidance in their lives. Later, the mothers of the Oratory School Boys gave tribute to Newman with a heartfelt speech and a present. The next day, the school's teachers and students paid their respects and welcomed his appointment as cardinal.

There were other events of particular relevance to Morgan that happened in that period, with some of them relating to Newman. Perhaps the most significant was his visit to Rome in early 1880, accompanying Fr. John Norris, the then Father Prefect of the school. Both were received in private audience by Pope Leo XIII. Norris described the visit in a letter to Newman:

> We have had our audience – and such an audience – we had the Pope all to ourselves for 10 minutes in his little room and we have both come away delighted and enchanted with the Holy Father's kindness and sweetness and his condescension and still more pleased with his evident love of you.[11]

After their return from Rome, Norris and Morgan (who acted as sacristan and attendant) accompanied Newman to Norfolk House, home of the Duke of Norfolk in London, between May 8th and May 15th 1880. This visit was a homage from British society (not only Catholics) to his appointment as cardinal. Norfolk House remained open all that week, some days hosting up to 400 visitors, allowing Morgan to meet and socialise with the most distinguished English Roman Catholics of the time.

The Catholic newspaper, *The Tablet*, described what happened those days in Norfolk House:

---

supposed to ask for privileges" but immediately he said, "Denis, you may go to Rednal, but stay one week. It will do you good".

10. A vestment which may most conveniently be described as a long liturgical mantle, open in front and fastened at the breast with a band or clasp.

11. Charles Stephen Dessain, (Ed.), *The Letters and Diaries of John Henry Newman. Vol., XXIX*, Thomas Nelson and Sons Ltd, Edinburgh, 1961, p. 228.

The Duke and Duchess of Norfolk had a dinner party at Norfolk House, St James's Square, on Monday evening, when their guests included his Eminence Cardinal Newman, the Duke and Duchess of Bedford, the Marquis and Marchioness of Salisbury, Lady Mary Fitzalan Howard, the Earl of Denbigh, the Earl of Kenmare, the Earl and Countess of Glasgow, Viscount and Viscountess Campden, Viscount and Viscountess Enfield, Lady Victoria Kirwan, Lady Amabel Kerr, Lord Ronald Gower, the Bishop of Southwark, Lord and Lady Herries, Lord and Lady Hylton, Lord and Lady Churston, Lord Lyons, Rt. Hon. A. Beresford-Hope, Sir George Bowyer, Bart., Mr and Mrs George Lane-Fox, Rev. F. Morris, **Rev. F. Morgan** and Mr Wilfrid Wilberforce. On Tuesday their Graces received at dinner his Eminence Cardinal Newman, the Duchess of Westminster, Lady Phillippa Fitzalan Howard, Lady Margaret Fitzalan Howard, Lord and Lady Edmund Talbot, Earl Granville, the Earl of Ashburnham, the Earl and Countess of Jersey, Lord and Lady Arundell of Wardour, Lord and Lady Howard of Glossop, Lord Emly, Lord Norreys, the Bishop of Amycla, Hon. and Right Rev. Monsignor Talbot, Hon. William H. and Mrs North, Miss Minna Hope, Miss Kirwan, Mr and Mrs Francis Kerr, Mrs Washington Hibbert, Mr Wegg-Prosser, Mr Edward Hope, Mr Basil Wilberforce, Mr and Mrs Lilly, Mr. E. Bellasis, Rev. F. Norris, **Rev. F. Morgan**, and Mr E. G. Ward. On Thursday also the Duke and Duchess entertained guests at dinner, and on each of Monday, Tuesday and Thursday evenings the Duchess had a small and early reception. On Friday there was an afternoon reception. Cardinal Newman was to leave town for Birmingham today (Saturday).[12]

In the following years, Francis Morgan remained a novice, until he was finally ordained as a priest on March the 4th 1883 and shortly after joined the Community of the Oratory, on May the 25th.

He had a whole life ahead to devote to his vocation.

---

12. *The Tablet*. 15th May 1880, p. 24.

The Community of the Oratory

The ordinary life of a member of the Community of the Birmingham Oratory was calm but not idle. Each member had his own room, which served as study and bedroom. All were very similar, with a crucifix over the bed dominating the chamber and the personal belongings and awards of the owner distributed along the sidewalls. Francis Morgan's room, which he called his "cell" was always crammed, largely due to a huge moving bookcase in the central part of the room, crammed with books, many of which were in Spanish.

Besides the rooms, there were several common spaces such as the library, which contained valuable books, several of them owned by Newman, or the refectory, a room with small tables and a pulpit in a corner, where they had their main meals. During dinner, the Superior sat alone (at least during Newman's epoch) whereas the other members of the Community sat two-by-two. The food was served by two Fathers while a novice read a chapter of the Bible from the pulpit, followed by a text from the life of St Philip Neri, and finally a passage belonging to any book, religious or profane, of general interest. On finishing dinner, one Father would propose two issues for discussion or, rather, for an exchange of views. They would then move into another room where they had a frugal dessert and a glass of wine.

The Community, following St Philip's rules, was a congregation of secular priests who were obedient, but bound by no vows. This justifies the long novitiate of three years, which necessarily tested the resolve of the individual looking to join a community without vows. The Superior, or Provost, was elected every three years by way of vote, along with four deputies to help him in governing the Community. However, not all Fathers had the right to vote, as this was restricted to those who had been members of the congregation for ten or more years. These members were known as the decennial Fathers.

The Provost didn't have the right to decide any serious matters related to the Community on his own. In such cases the issue was resolved by the general congregation though, as previously mentioned, only the decennial Fathers could ultimately vote. This was the case when, due to disputes with the first Father Prefect, Nicholas Darnell, in the Oratory School, Newman (then Provost) needed the support of the Fathers of the Oratory in order to replace him.

Admission to the congregation also required a vote from the decennial Fathers. Moreover, the candidate needed to be between eighteen and forty years and possess sufficient income to maintain himself. As stated earlier, it was necessary to undergo a novitiate of three years, followed by a ten-year stay in the Community before being able to vote or become eligible for positions of importance in the congregation.

The three objectives pursued by the Community were prayer, sacraments and preaching. The first implied special care was taken when carrying out liturgical services. Sacraments had to be frequently received by members of the Community. In particular, confession carried great importance, hence one of the Fathers was required to sit daily in the confessional. Following the teachings of St Philip, gentleness rather than severity prevailed in any advice that the priests gave. Preaching was also an important element and sermons were personal and simple to understand.

The Birmingham Oratory was in all aspects a parish. Above all concerns, there were daily Masses and confessions, but the Fathers also preached and helped in prisons, hospices and orphanages, along with maintaining and managing free schools for the poor. However, the Oratory had some unique characteristics. Since there was no requirement for its members to renounce their temporal possessions (most of them came from wealthy families), it contrasted sharply with other orders.

It was not a question being boastful, but access to their own incomes allowed them to fulfil certain wishes, such as taking vacations, providing donations for the choir, or intervening in delicate financial matters; Morgan himself was able to give economic support to the Tolkien brothers. However, despite their social activities, pastoral life was the guiding principle of this community and they were entirely devoted to this task.

Regarding Morgan's career in the Community, during his novitiate in the early eighties, he served as personal secretary to Cardinal Newman, who even wrote to him in Port St Mary in the summer of 1882. The purpose of this was to provide him with guidelines for his duties during the Cardinal's absences from the Oratory. Among these, he was required to check if there were donations included in any of the letters sent to the Cardinal and hand them to Fr. Austin Henry Mills (the then Treasurer of the Community). He even had to respond to some of these letters, especially a couple from the authors Aubrey Thomas de Vere and Alfred Tennyson, confirming the Cardinal's return date.

Later on, he was with Newman in London for a short stint. One year before the Cardinal's death, Morgan accompanied him to mediate in a dispute at the Cadbury's Chocolate factory between the Quaker owners and their workers, who were mostly Irish Catholics.

Over time, he held other positions within the congregation under the remit of Father Minister. As such, he was responsible for dealing with the domestic staff working at the Oratory (the Community as well as the School). He was usually helped in this by a novice, or the Church Treasurer; every Monday, in the sacristy, he counted all the collected alms (at that time, totalling around £35). He also acted on behalf of the Oratory in several other issues, acting as its representative for some of the donations provided by the Community. At one point, he helped promote a proposal to Edward Ilsley, Bishop of Birmingham, on the management of the female schools linked to the Oratory.

Indeed, he showed a keen interest in educational issues from his early years as a priest. His presence can be found in various meetings on Catholic education, and also in the distribution of prizes and the exhibition days at different Catholic schools. It is a verifiable fact that he visited distant schools like Abbey School (next to Loch Ness), St Anne's Catholic Primary School in Birmingham, St Mary's College, Oscott, etc.

He also participated in religious activities; for instance, he repeatedly attended the annual pilgrimage to Erdington Abbey, as well as presiding over the opening of a number of Catholic churches, and was present at several official tributes to Catholic personalities. Obviously, he also exercised his priesthood and administered the sacraments many times during his lengthy ministry. As such, he oversaw and assisted in numerous weddings, baptisms and funerals.

It's clear that he was never a man who sought notoriety, as demonstrated by how few references there are to his jobs, despite his seniority in the order. He wasn't particularly outstanding in sports, nor was he an inspirational speaker or writer, but he certainly wasn't ignorant; his room full of books attest to his obvious love of reading and knowledge.

Undoubtedly, Morgan played his part in the shaping and development of the Birmingham Oratory, though he was mainly remembered for more anecdotal matters, such as his interest in the choir and singing. He described boys with good singing voices as "drops of liquid gold"[1]. At the same time, he was regularly involved as a tenor at sung Masses, which were usually performed at Easter or on other special occasions like All Saints' Day.

In any case, his dedication to tasks that didn't bring intellectual recognition probably contributed to the fact that his achievements aren't well known or highlighted. His main activities were pastoral, such as taking confession, visiting parishioners, or collaborating at the annual bazaar in support of the parochial school. In fact, his care for the children who attended the school is highlighted in his obituary in *The Tablet*:

---

1. F. Philip Lynch, 'Francis Xavier Morgan (1935)', Chapter address on 16th November 1987, *Birmingham Oratory*, <http://www.birminghamoratory.org.uk/about-the-oratory/biographies-of-past-members/f-francis-xavier-morgan-1935> [accessed 12 December 2017].

He was attracted especially to work for the children in the parochial school. To these little ones he was devoted, and for them he did much good educational work.²

On the other hand, his obituary in the *Oratory School Magazine* highlights his personality and temperament:

He was always ready to cheer every one with his hearty laugh and witty remarks, or to console them with good advice and words of encouragement.³

This also points to another of his virtues, which afforded him some unexpected recognition:

He will long be remembered for his many deeds of charity, all done in the most unassuming and secret way.⁴

Despite his many years in the congregation, he never became Provost (the leader of the Community), a position that was usually occupied by veteran priests. After Newman, Morgan saw the elections of Fathers Ignatius Ryder, John Norris, Richard Bellasis, Denis Sheil (Bellasis and Sheil studied at the Oratory School) and Vincent Reade to this post.

The death of Cardinal Newman, after many years of friendship, was a major blow to Morgan and the other Fathers. Indeed, Newman's latter years were marked by his failing health due to old age. Among the Fathers of the Oratory, this was a constant concern: his evident physical deterioration prevented him from performing his daily tasks or, for example, to attend Mass without assistance from several of the Fathers. In contrast, the Cardinal did fully retain his mental faculties until the end. In one of his last appearances, showing his continuous involvement with his work, he attended a play performed by the school students and presented the annual prizes. Just a few days after this, his health suffered a fatal dip, due to pneumonia, which caused a high fever and he fell into a coma.

Fr. Austin Mills administered the last rites in the presence of the fourteen members of the Community, who went on to witness his death on August 11th 1890. His body was displayed at the Church of the Oratory until the day of his funeral, on August 19th. It was visited by large crowds, under the vigilant watch of all the Fathers. The funeral services included a solemn Pontifical Mass and Requiem at the Oratory Church, followed by a shorter

---

2. *The Tablet*, June 22nd 1935, p 12.
3. *Oratory School Magazine* 89, December 1935, p 10.
4. Op. cit. The most memorable example was the case of Tolkien's brothers, as discussed below. Morgan increased the limited amount of money they had inherited with his own income. This gave them, without their knowledge, greater economic security.

funeral service in Rednal, where Newman was buried alongside previously deceased members of the Community. More than fifteen thousand people accompanied the funeral procession on its journey from the Oratory to the cemetery in Rednal.

Life moved on and Morgan was involved in several notable events that followed Newman's death, such as the construction of the new church (the foundation stone was laid in 1903 and the church was solemnly opened in December 1909). He also took part in the controversial Oratory School move, after the Great War, from its original location, next to the Oratory, to Caversham Park, Reading. Morgan visited the school at its new location every year in June or July. His presence was celebrated and deeply missed after his death.[5]

Unlike some of his colleagues (an example being Fr. Joseph Bacchus who, despite his inspiring sermons, was unable to hold a conversation while visiting a private home), Morgan had a cheerful temperament and the ability to communicate easily, and even to gossip. This was surely his most distinguishing feature. Perhaps one of the most accurate descriptions of him came from J.R.R. Tolkien who, in a letter written in 1965, thirty years after Morgan's death, says:

> He was an upper-class Welsh-Spaniard Tory, and seemed to some just a pottering old snob and gossip. He was – and he was not. I first learned charity and forgiveness from him; and in the light of it pierced even the "liberal"[6] darkness out of which I came.[7]

---

5. He loved the school very much and even employed the term "earthly paradise" to refer to it. *Oratory School Magazine* 89, December 1935, p. 10.

6. In this context, Morgan becomes a link with the teachings of Cardinal Newman, who expressed unequivocally his ideas on this regard in his first speech as cardinal: "For thirty, forty, fifty years I have resisted to the best of my powers the spirit of liberalism in religion. [...] Liberalism in religion is the doctrine that there is no positive truth in religion, but that one creed is as good as another, and this is the teaching which is gaining substance and force daily. It is inconsistent with any recognition of any religion, as true. It teaches that all are to be tolerated, for all are matters of opinion. Revealed religion is not a truth, but a sentiment and a taste; not an objective fact, not miraculous; and it is the right of each individual to make it say just what strikes his fancy." *Speech of His Eminence Cardinal Newman on the reception of the "Biglietto" at Cardinal Howard's palace in Rome on the 12th of May 1879*, Libreria Spithöver, Rome, 1879, pp. 6-7.

7. Humphrey Carpenter, (ed.), *The Letters of J.R.R. Tolkien*, Houghton Mifflin, Boston, 1981, Letter 267, p 354.

Life Between Birmingham and Port St Mary

In the early 20th century, a local journalist from Port St Mary, called Mariano López Muñoz, stated in the *Revista Portuense*:

> In our town exists a spiritual legacy, but not an ethnic heritage. Port St Mary is not the race, nor the root or trunk of a family. The city has more alembics than cradles. When one milligram of sea salt, which saturates the atmosphere, or a drop of subtle wine from the soleras, which numbs but does not inebriate, penetrates into the blood, Port St Mary has completed its conquest. A child of Castilians or Cantabrians born here always says that he is "Portuense"[1], as too would the grandson of an Englishman or other foreigner.[2]

These words are not simply a passionate attempt to exalt the virtues of his town, because there is an element of truth to it which can be proved empirically, with Francis Morgan providing a good example. Although his evolution from the young Curro Morgan to Fr. Francis Morgan increased the distance between him and his family, friends and childhood, and knowing that he spent his adult life far from Port St Mary, Morgan always referred to the city where he was born as "home". In letters he sent to people in the town, he would commonly finish off by wishing the best to "the ones from home", which was certainly more than a formality, and showed where he placed his roots.

On the other hand, he never intended to forget his origins or abandon them. He was different from his Oratorian colleagues because of his sunny and jovial disposition, which was unconventional for an English archetype, and something he attributed to his Spanish origins. In fact, while he was still able, he visited Spain and used his holidays to periodically return to his "tribe", as he called his Spanish family and friends.

It is interesting to reflect on his feelings of nostalgia, as one residing far from his family and the landscapes of southern Spain, despite living as a native in England and being well versed in the country's customs and language. In any case, this shouldn't be misconstrued, or give the impression

---

1. Demonym of Port St Mary.
2. The *Revista Portuense* was a local newspaper from Port St Mary, published between 1890 and 1938, whose head office was at 116 Larga Street. Its news usually focused on the social life and events of the city, or neighboring towns, although sometimes reproduced national and even international news. (Translated by the author of this work).

that there were any doubts about his vocation, which never faltered.

Morgan's bonds with Port St Mary, beyond his family and properties, were certainly solid. Francis Morgan (senior) was considered a great man in the city. He, for example, was a founding member, in 1852, of the *Casino Portuense*, along with the most prominent figures of the town. The *Casino Portuense* was a kind of civic society that served as a meeting place for its members, where gatherings, lectures, and even parties took place.

Throughout the 1860s to '70s, the family's presence in the city was significantly reduced, due to many of them habitually residing abroad. In fact, María Manuela didn't even return to Spain after the death of her husband in 1876, but instead moved to the south of London, in Richmond. However, the oldest of Morgan's brothers, Tomás, settled in the two family houses in Port St Mary. A short time later, the *Casino Portuense* established its headquarters in one of these houses, on the ground floor of the house at 124 Larga Street (it was also accessible from Nevería Street), where it remained until 1899.

In those days, the future of his brothers began to take shape. Shortly after their father's death, Francis started his novitiate at the Birmingham Oratory (as discussed in previous chapters) and Augusto began his long business career. Meanwhile, his sister Isabel joined the religious order of the Sisters of Marie Reparatrice, spending much of her life in the Holy Land.

Augusto Morgan moved away from Port St Mary for several years. It seems that he didn't return until the death of his brother Tomás (coinciding with the end of the First World War). He inherited the family houses from him which, as firstborn, Tomás had inherited from their mother.

Augusto firstly resided in London and, when his mother died in April 1894, he hurried to Port St Mary (unlike his brother Francis, who couldn't go to Spain). The year 1894 took on special significance as a result of this death, and the three brothers met at the family home in August. Indeed, a sad story, published on August 18th in the *Revista Portuense*, confirms Francis Morgan's presence in the city. He had to take confession and deliver last rites to an Irish girl named Isabel Byan, who fell ill while spending the summer at Port St Mary.

If we follow Augusto Morgan's path, it should be noted that, in the late 19th century, he changed his residence to Porto, in northern Portugal where, in 1898, several members of the family relaunched the Morgan family business (which, at that time, also had offices in Spain and England). They established a new company, formally named Morgan Brothers (Wine Shippers) Limited, with an initial capital of 100,000 British Pounds.

Augusto's participation in this business, and other ventures that he undertook, is particularly relevant because Francis Morgan's capital was quite liberally overseen by his brother. In fact, the yields from the businesses with which Augusto was involved (along with returns from his investments) were his main source of income. Oddly, as his name didn't usually appear in the legal records for these, Francis Morgan had to pay taxes to inherit his own money after the Augusto's death. He complained of this in a letter to his second nephew, Antonio Osborne:

> You must know that almost all the capital I possess, on which Augusto paid me annual interest, is included in the calculation of his property, so I'm paying taxes on what is and has been my property over the years.[3]

Returning to Morgan Brothers Ltd, its managers resided in Portugal and England. Its first executive director, Albert Morgan, a cousin, and son of Thomas Morgan Jr, married the daughter of John Alexander Fladgate, who was one of Porto's leading producers. The other major partners, aside from Augusto Morgan, were Aaron Herbert Morgan (Albert's brother), and Ivo Bligh, who was the only owner who wasn't a member of the Morgan family. Bligh would become, after the death of his father, the eighth Earl of Darnley, although he was well-known for captaining the England cricket team that beat Australia in 1882-83, in the now-famous Ashes Test series.

Early in the 20th century, Augusto Morgan took over the management of the company, which he combined with an active social life, becoming member of the executive committee of the prestigious Oporto British Club. He was succeeded as manager by a young relative named James Morgan (son of Ernest, a brother of Albert and Aaron Herbert), who was the last member of the Morgan family to lead the company. The 1930s to '40s saw the drastic decline of Morgan Brothers Ltd., and the firm, no longer belonging to the family, was finally absorbed by Croft in the early fifties.

During his years of residence in Porto, Augusto frequently travelled to Spain and sometimes brought his brother Thomas back with him to spend time together. When he finally returned home to Spain, he actively engaged in social and religious acts as a distinguished member of the *Archicofradía del Santísimo* (Confraternity of the Blessed Sacrament), as a member of the board of directors of the Catholic Social House, as a generous contributor on the restoration of the organ and bells of the *Iglesia Prioral* of Port St Mary and, in the final years of his life, as president of the Employers Board. But his return didn't signal the end of his vocation for business: in 1921, when a branch of *Banco Matritense* opened in the city, he was appointed as its president, a post he held until the closure of the firm in 1923.

Francis Morgan found it harder to travel home than Augustus, given his obligations as a member of the Oratory, but his summer visits were frequent,

---

3. Francis Morgan letter to Antonio Osborne, February 17th 1933, Osborne Archive. (Translated by the author of this work).

even though it was not an easy or comfortable trip. It required him going from Birmingham to a coastal city, where he would board a ship belonging to any of the companies that made the journey to the Iberian Peninsula, generally to Gibraltar (one of the most popular shipping companies was the *Peninsular & Oriental Steam Navigation Company*, better known as P&O). The sea voyage between England and Gibraltar consisted of about five days sailing on the open sea. From there, a long stagecoach trip, or a journey of several hours on a ferry to Cadiz, finally took him home.[4]

In a way, these recurring trips were an escape from the urban life of industrial Birmingham. The evident contrast between the two was especially evident in the form of technical advances; some as important as electricity, or the appearance of cars, which happened in the great English city earlier than in southern Spain.

His summer stays allowed him to visit nearby destinations, where the family spent their holidays while his great-grandmother was alive, such as Chiclana or, in the hinterlands, Arcos de la Frontera, or Bornos. However, what mattered most to him was being back in Port St Mary, which still retained, save for a few changes, its original appearance and the fundamental elements that gave the town its unique personality. Being there offered him the opportunity to share in the lives of his relatives, and an incessant flow of weddings, births, and deaths. Among those who passed away, we should specifically note those of his great-aunt Cecilia[5], in 1877, the celebrity of the family thanks to her novels, and the death of his uncle Tomás Osborne Böhl de Faber, the patriarch of the Osborne family, in 1890.

At this time, around the turn of the century, the Osbornes broke almost completely away from their English past and sold their lands in Devon, which had been inherited from Thomas Osborne-Mann. They did, however, maintain the tradition of sending their children to be educated in England. Interestingly, Francis Morgan was required to take care of small needs associated with them, being something of a family representative in the British Isles.

Among his "tasks", he would accompany them to Spain for holidays, if their holidays coincided, as was the case, for example, in the summer of 1911. While his English wards, the Tolkiens, enjoyed a memorable holiday in Switzerland, he accompanied Ignacio Osborne Vázquez, aged thirteen, to Spain, the boy who, a few years later, would inherit leadership of the business and run it for half a century.

---

4. In 1875 an English traveller called Henry Vizetelly thoroughly described this trip, whose account is the starting point for his work *Facts about Sherry Gleaned in the Vinegards and Bodegas of the Jerez, Seville, Moguer, & Montilla Districts during the Autumn of 1875*.

5. Some of the writer's personal belongings were finally inherited by Morgan because his mother, María Manuela Osborne, as her niece, was among her heirs. She received from her, in addition to 1,000 Spanish reales (old Spanish coin), a bracelet of gold and a figure of Our Lady of Sorrows.

Some interesting details of an incident are described in a letter (still preserved) which Morgan wrote in early 1914 to Elisa Vázquez, his cousin Tomas Osborne Guezala's wife, where Ignacio, their son, is again the main focus. He was studying at Beaumont[6] and travelled to London with his brother José Luis (also a pupil at this school) in order to treat a tendon injury. There, waiting for them, was Francis Morgan, who had found a specialist. He took Ignacio to see the famous "bonesetter", Herbert Atkinson Barker, a manipulative surgeon without a medical degree, who was nevertheless very popular among the London upper classes. Afterwards, he also had to attend to some of the boys' needs:

> Ignacio said to me that he needed a coat and other things and I have bought them for him, but José Luis, as always, did not need anything. But he also had no money for small personal expenses, so I gave them both some.[7]

These family obligations were rather anecdotal in relation to his life in England, where he spent most of his life. There he developed his vocation and exercised his priesthood, but he still had time to travel, and even take vacations and tour the country. In fact, some photos of his travels are still preserved to this day, such as one from August 1890 (shortly after the death of Cardinal Newman), taken at Lynton, a small town in the coast of Devon with several beautiful spots. He was accompanied by a boy, who was probably a pupil at the Oratory School.

Still, as we have noted before, his real "home" was Port St Mary. It isn't hard to imagine him wandering the streets of his hometown during summer evenings, or strolling along one of the main roads of the town, such as Palacios Street. This street starts at the *Iglesia Prioral* square, the location of many family baptisms, weddings and burials. It reaches almost as far as the pier, finishing at the entrance of the *San Juan de Dios* Hospital, which is next to the Guadalete river.

Cutting through Palacios Street are Larga Street and Nevería Street (called Castelar[8] for some time, though it is now named Muñoz Seca[9]), like two parallel lines, perpendicularly traversing the city centre area. The Morgan family houses were on these streets, in two connecting buildings

---

6. As his father did before him.
7. Francis Morgan letter to Elisa Vázquez, February 29th 1914, Osborne Archive. (Translated by the author of this work).
8. Emilio Castelar (1832-1899). Spanish politician who was the last president of the First Spanish Republic.
9. Pedro Muñoz Seca (1879-1936). Spanish playwright born in Port St Mary, who died in the first months of the Spanish Civil War. His family home was in the same street, at number 48. It's like his family and the Morgans knew each other because, in addition to their mutual neighborhood, members of the Muñoz family belonged to the Casino's board of directors. This also applies to the family of the most famous writer in the history of the town, the poet Rafael Alberti (1902-1999), who lived nearby, and whose grandparents were founding members of the Casino.

bound by Palacios Street and Santo Domingo Street. Close by, turning to the left, at 57 Palacios Street, is the Osborne house, where today a plaque commemorates Washington Irving's[10] stay here and, a little further down, we arrive again at the *Iglesia Prioral*.

On Nevería Street, just a few meters from Morgan's house, is the Carmelite convent. There, in a family vault, most of the family members are buried (not only Morgans, but also Osbornes), including María Manuela and his sons, Tomás and Augusto. Distanced a little from these places is the imposing presence *San Marcos* Castle, witness to the city's ancient times. Near the castle stands the Osborne wineries and, at 4 Fernán Caballero Street, the "Casa de Vicuña y Campillo", the mansion where the family patriarch usually resided. Further away stands the impressive bullring which, well into the 20th century, was the border between the old city and the depopulated zone, where urban growth would take place.

---

10. This is highly unlikely because, as has been noted, he was in *El Cerrillo*.

Maturity

The Tolkiens

In the early 20th century, Fr. Francis Morgan became parish priest for the Church of the Oratory. He regularly socialised with the parishioners, trying to help them with their problems, and visited them to give spiritual and human support. In fact, given that English Roman Catholics were a minority, and a marginalised group who suffered widespread disaffection from the Anglican majority, the bond between them and their priest was essential to keeping alive the flames of faith.

It might be thought of as an important change for him be so directly in contact with the parishioners, many of whom belonged to the lowlier classes. By contrast, his best friends, who were mainly from among his relations or those he had met at the Oratory School (classmates or pupils who knew him when he was already a member of the Community), enjoyed high social positions.

His other English relatives, apart from the members of the Morgan family, were the Shaws and the Galtons, all of whom belonged to the social elite. In the mid-nineteenth century, the Shaw family was headed up by Charles James Shaw and his wife Nerea, née Rücker Álvarez de Navia, who he had met and married in Uruguay, though her family, on her father's side, were from Hamburg. They moved to Birmingham years later, which was the native habitat of Charles James, who was a prosperous merchant. Their sons, Charles Conrad and James Frederick,[1] born in 1857 and 1858 respectively, studied at the Oratory School at the same time as Francis Morgan, which cemented their friendship.

As a priest, Morgan participated in many of his family's events, such as the wedding of James Frederick Shaw in 1890, where he gave the works of Cardinal Newman as a present to him, and the funeral of Nerea Shaw in 1891. His contact with them was maintained over the years, and he even helped conduct, as an old man, the funeral of James Frederick's only son, in 1930. Among the Galtons, who have already been mentioned in previous chapters, there were also prominent members of British society. In fact, a member of the family was (from the non-Catholic branch) Francis Galton, the famous English scientist who was related to Charles Darwin and the

---

1. James Frederick Shaw was High Sheriff of Warwickshire between 1909 and 1910. His brother, Charles Conrad Shaw, made a large donation for the new church of the Oratory and because of its numerous actions and donations in favour of the Catholic Church he was honored by the Pope with the Order of St Sylvester.

Barclay bankers. In the Catholic branch, the patriarch was Theodore H. Galton, who died in 1881. Morgan, who was still a novice, collaborated in conducting his funeral Mass.

With regards to his relationships outside of his family, he had several illustrious classmates. As a member of the Community, he also worked with the Oratory School and socialised with some of the young people there who, over time, became men who would play prominent roles in their society. Several of these were devoted to politics or diplomacy and, despite being Catholics, reached important positions. Some examples were James Fitzalan Hope, Philip Henry Kerr, and Pierse Creagh Loftus. Many of the others joined the army, like Lieutenant General Sir Adrian Carton de Wiart, while some even became spies, such as Edward Noel. The list of former pupils contemporary to Morgan also includes scientists, like Charles John Philip Cave, musicians like Arthur Hervey or the famous tenor, Gervase Elwes, painters like John Reinhard Weguelin, and writers like Hilaire Belloc, who was one of the most academically outstanding students from the school (he won awards in mathematics and literature and years later achieved great fame as an author).

Despite appearances, right from when Morgan became an Oratorian, due in large part to his personality and natural generosity, he was connected also to parishioners who weren't as fortunate as his friends and acquaintances. Given that he already collaborated with the parish, the mission schools and the Oratory's solidarity projects, he had no problems when he began his new role as a parish priest. It must not be forgotten that, as noted above, the position of Catholics in society was more complicated than it might seem, because they ran counter to the general inertia. Among them, the worst to suffer were those who had converted from Anglicanism, as they had to overcome their own personal *journey through the desert*, metaphorically speaking.

Through this, Morgan met a family whose members included a young widow named Mabel Tolkien and her two small sons, named Ronald and Hilary, aged eight and six years at the time. Mabel's (née Suffield) deceased husband, Arthur, had been the manager of a bank in the south of Africa. He died suddenly, while she and the children had been spending some time in England. Mabel and her children were in a delicate economic situation, although their real troubles arose from religious disagreements with their relatives.

The Suffields and the Tolkiens formed an amalgam of Protestant beliefs, composed of Baptists, Methodists and Anglicans strongly linked to their community. None of them belonged to the Roman Catholic Church. In this context, Mabel and her children's conversion in 1900 was like a family earthquake.

Pressures immediately mounted. Her sister May, who had dared to take this step with her, had to renounce her new faith because her husband forbade her to ever enter a Catholic church again. Mabel was shunned by almost all of her relations (and also those of her late husband); grandparents and uncles alike firmly rejected her conversion and thus withdrew financial support for her family. Rather than being intimidated, Mabel Tolkien remained faithful to her decision.

In early 1902, she and her children moved to a modest house in Oliver Road, near the Oratory. Before then, they had lived for four years in Sarehole, a hamlet near Birmingham and, later, briefly, in the suburbs of Moseley and King's Head. The help Mabel received from the Oratory, in particular from Fr. Morgan, whose visits to Oliver Road soon became a common occurrence, was crucial in many respects. Most importantly, Mabel and her sons found a place where they were finally welcomed, after being marginalised by almost all their relatives. Several reasons could explain the harmony between Morgan and the Tolkien family. Surely one of the most significant is the fact that he, who was coincidentally of the same age as the late Arthur Tolkien, felt great love for the children, and the thought of the young Tolkiens in dire straits on account of religious differences surely tugged at his heartstrings.

Both boys had been educated by their mother, until Ronald, the eldest, attended the prestigious, and expensive, King Edward's School, in the heart of Birmingham. However, Mabel was unable to meet the expenses of the school and Ronald was moved to St Philip's Grammar School[2] where, thanks to Morgan's intervention, he had secured a place. Nevertheless, he only attended for a very short period, as he won a scholarship and returned to King Edward's soon after.

Some years before these events, the Tolkiens and the Suffields had been relatively well-off families, whose fortunes had grown in parallel to the industrial development of the 19th century Birmingham area. Even though they were far removed from the privileged social circle of the Morgans, it would be inaccurate to consider them as lower class families.

The Tolkiens owned their own family business for many years, with the profits allowing Arthur to study at King Edward's School without having to face the hardships that his children had to. However, its bankruptcy led to him seeking fortune in Africa, where he later died. Meanwhile, the Suffields had run a prosperous drapery business, which allowed them to give their children a good education. Still, they also eventually faced severe economic problems and had to abandon their once thriving business.

Although living in a diminished financial situation, the help of both

---

2. Although linked to the Oratory, it should not be confused with the Oratory School.

families had been valuable in assisting the young widow, Mabel Tolkien, and her two children. However, after their conversion, this economic support became minimal and, eventually, religious differences led to a split between the families, and the Oratory became their shelter. Besides being their church, it was also a place where children could receive love and attention, while socialising with other Community parishioners and priests. For example, in 1903, one of the young priests taught Ronald to play chess. During Christmas of that same year, the boy took his First Communion.

Unfortunately, tragic events quickly followed, and 1904 became a sorrowful year. Mabel had been sick since late 1903, though doctors were unable to determine her disease; in early 1904, she was finally diagnosed with diabetes. At that time, there was no treatment for this condition, so it was invariably fatal because of that, and Mabel was expected to live for a couple of years at most. As a result, the family was temporarily fractured; they left the Oliver Road house and, while Mabel was in hospital, she sent her two children to live with relatives.[3]

By the summer, she had recovered slightly and was reunited with her children. The family moved from the city to the countryside, thanks again to the help of Fr. Morgan, who found accommodation for them. He made the necessary arrangements, so they could live in a nice, quiet place, ideal for Mabel's recovery. It was located in Rednal, south-west of Birmingham. There, about ten miles from the Oratory, at the foot of the Lickey Hills, the Oratorians owned a house with a small chapel which served as a retreat. The Community's cemetery was beside the house, where its deceased members were buried, including Cardinal Newman. This rural property had been acquired in the mid-nineteenth century, thanks to donations received from the Catholic community of New York.

It was quite common for Morgan to go there on vacation, if only for a few days. In fact, there is a photograph of him in the verandah of the house, with its walls covered in ivy. He also kept an Irish terrier there called Lord Roberts, in tribute to Field Marshal Frederick Sleigh Roberts, an Anglo-Irish military liberator of Bloemfontein[4] during the Boer War.

There was a cottage near the Oratory Retreat in those days, known as "Woodside", which belonged to the local postman, Mr Till. The arrangement was that he and his wife would rent a room to the Tolkiens and the lady of the house would take care of household tasks, such as cleaning and meal preparation. It was a simple life, and while the children enjoyed the bucolic lifestyle, their mother recovered in a healthy environment.

---

3. It is sadly curious that Mabel suffer from a disease that was common among Fr. Morgan's family. It seems certain that at least his great-grandfather, Juan Nicolás Böhl de Faber (it is highly likely that he died as a result of this illness), and his great aunt, Cecilia, had diabetes.
4. Bloemfontein is the city where the Tolkien brothers were born.

On Sundays they attended Mass in the nearby town of Bromsgrove with Mr and Mrs Church, an elderly servant couple who lived at the retreat. They were very affectionate with the children. He was a veteran of the Crimean War. Mrs Church left an indelible impression on Hilary Tolkien with the delicious "damson cheese" she would make for them - years later, he said that it was the best he had ever tasted and he expected her to continue cooking it for the angels in heaven.[5]

The summer was pleasant, especially for the boys. It was an environment opposite to the city, with the nearby hills and woods ideal for their games. In fact, they spent much of their time climbing trees, in particular a favourite sycamore, and competing with squirrels to collect and eat their fruits. Morgan visited them frequently during this period. It wasn't uncommon to see him playing with the children and helping them fly their kites; in the serenity of that peaceful time, they discovered an little known fact him; a hidden hobby he practiced only on rare occasions: pipe smoking using a large cherry-wood pipe. This memory fascinated Ronald Tolkien, who years later confessed that this might be the source of his own penchant for pipe smoking.[6]

Sometimes Morgan's duties prevented him from visiting Rednal, which displeased the young Ronald Tolkien. He therefore decided to write Morgan a coded letter, a sort of cryptogram formed of simple drawings, letters and numbers (perhaps it is more appropriate to refer to it as a "rebus puzzle"), expressing his discontent. This letter, dated August 8th 1904, is preserved in the Bodleian Library, although it has also been published separately in two fragments.[7]

It is possible to decipher the message using a series of imaginative matches. For example, the address is represented by a combination of a drawing of a forest, the letter "S", a single eye and "500 E". In the next line, there is a drawing of a country house, followed by "N A 50" in red. Thus, interpreting the numbers as Roman numerals (500=D and 50=L), the forest as representing "wood", the eye as "I", the country house as "cottage", and the red-inked "N A 50" as an adjective, we get: WOOD S I D E - COTTAGE - RED N A L.

Using this method, the full message could be:

---

[5]. Hilary Tolkien, *Black and White Ogre Country: The Lost Tales of Hilary Tolkien*, ADC Publications Ltd, Moreton-in-Marsh, 2009, p. 26.
[6]. Humphrey Carpenter, *JRR Tolkien – A Biography*, George Allen & Unwin, London, 1977, p. 30.
[7]. The front of the letter is reproduced in Judith Priestman, *J.R.R. Tolkien: Life and Legend: An Exhibition to Commemorate the Centenary of the Birth of J.R.R. Tolkien (1892-1973)*, Bodleian Library, Oxford, 1992, p. 17, and the back in John and Priscilla Tolkien, *The Tolkien Family Album*, Houghton Mifflin, Boston, p. 22.

Woodside Cottage. Rednal

My dear wise owl, Fr. Francis,
you are too bad
not to come, in
spite of Fr. Denis[8].
I am so sorry you
did not like the
word "piano" in my
last letter so I
am sending you
one all pictures.
We each have
found two lovely
walks to take you
when you do
come out here
which we hope
will be soon.
Your loving
Ronald

After the pictures, the letter ends with a limerick:

There was an old priest named Francis
Who was so fond of "cheefongy" dances
That he sat up too late
And worried his pate
Arranging these Frenchified Prances
(This is to pay you out for not coming,
and sending Father Edmund[9] instead).[10]

Both the encoded message and the limerick provide meaningful information about Ronald Tolkien's emerging talent for wordplay and invented alphabets. It also indicates how close Morgan was to the boys and a friendly complicity between them. It leads us to wonder about unknown summer adventures and numerous happy moments.

The Tolkiens' stay in Rednal extended beyond the end of that summer. Unfortunately, as the autumn progressed, Mabel's health inexorably worsened. Her children, just ten and twelve years old at the time, were

---

8. Fr. Denis Sheil (1865-1962). Quoted in previous chapters.
9. Fr. Edmund T. Hodgson. Born 1876.
10. Valuable information related to the interpretation of this codified letter is contained within the forums of the following website: *The Hall of Fire* <http://www.thehalloffire.net/forum/viewtopic.php?t=12> [accessed 12 December 2017].

probably unaware of this. Morgan, however, did realise her deteriorating condition and rightly worried about it, as Mabel had decided that, after her death, he would assume guardianship of the boys until they reached the age of majority.

In November, after a diabetic coma lasting six days, Mabel Tolkien died in Rednal. Only two people visited Mabel on her deathbed: her sister May, and the man who would henceforth act as guardian of her children: Fr. Francis Morgan.

Mabel was buried in the Catholic cemetery at Bromsgrove. Morgan took charge of the burial and placed a stone Celtic cross on her grave, of a kind that deceased priests buried in the Oratory cemetery had. Her burial was the first of the obligations he assumed in his mission of care for the boys.

A New Life

Mabel Tolkien bequeathed to her children a modest sum of money, mainly through shares in mining companies and African banks, and left them under the guardianship of Fr. Francis Morgan who, before her death, had proven his loyalty and his great affection for the children. There was also a practical component to this decision since, otherwise, their relatives would have taken the boys in and surely would have forced them to leave the Roman Catholic faith.

To deal with the legal matters pertaining to this, Morgan consulted Arthur J. O'Connor, a Catholic solicitor who had also been a student at the Oratory School. By March 1905, all of the shares (not a particularly substantial amount) came to Morgan, as Executor. Unexpectedly, Mabel's choice of guardian actually brought a greater profit to her children. Unbeknownst to them, they benefited from the generosity and economic capacity of their guardian; since Oratorians weren't required to give up their property or transfer their possessions to the Community, one of his first actions was to secretly increase the amount the boys inherited with funds from his own income.

Another issue he had to resolve was where the boys would live. They couldn't stay with relatives because this would give the appearance of handing them custody and condemning the boys to renouncing Catholicism. They couldn't reside at the Oratory either, as they weren't students at its school. The solution arrived in the form of Beatrice Suffield, née Barlett, who was recently widowed from William, one of Mabel's younger brothers (they both died in 1904). Aunt Beatrice lived near the Oratory, in a house on Stirling Road, just two hundred metres from Waterworks Road, the street where the famous Birmingham twin towers were erected (one of which is Perrott's Folly); these allegedly inspired Tolkien for his "Two Towers".

Beatrice wasn't averse to the children living with her and practising their religion but, in return, she demanded a monthly payment of four pounds and sixteen shillings, regardless of other expenditures that Morgan had to assume, extending beyond the boys' accommodation. Their aunt assigned a room for them but, apart from their school time, they were at the Oratory for most of the day. A typical day for them was taking turns serving at Fr. Morgan's early morning Mass, officiating at the Altar of Our Lady, followed by breakfast and playing with the cat who lived in the Oratory kitchen, before going to school. They also took part in parish activities and this was recorded in *The Parish Magazine*:

> Three patrols of Scouts under the Brothers Tolkien have been started, and they marched smartly in the wake of the Boys Brigade on Easter Monday. When they have done a little more drill, we shall ask some of our friends to help towards providing them with shirts, haversacks, etc.[1]

Hilary attended King Edward's School, as he had also received a scholarship there, so the brothers travelled together to the city centre. Under other circumstances, it might have seemed logical for them to change school and move to the Oratory School, or St Philip's Grammar School; both would have been more practical in many ways. However, Morgan's decision to put the quality of their education ahead of other criteria (King Edward's School was the best in the city and one of the best in the country) proved to be hugely successful. Tolkien recalled:

> Fr. Francis obtained permission for me to retain my scholarship at K[ing] E[dward's] S[chool] and continue there, and so I had the advantage of a (then) first rate school and that of a "good Catholic home"[2] – "in excelsis": virtually a junior inmate of the Oratory house, which contained many learned fathers (largely "converts").[3]

At school, the Tolkiens met youths from good families and different religions. Ronald cultivated a circle of friends with whom he would share further studies at the university, as well as the adversities of the First World War. Among them was Christopher Wiseman, who Morgan used to call "the grandson of The Pope of Wesley"[4] because his grandfather, Frederick Wiseman, was the President of the Wesleyan Methodist Conference.

Another important event which coincided with Morgan's guardianship of the Tolkien brothers was the construction and subsequent opening of the new church of the Oratory. For many years, the modest original church was intended to be replaced by a more prominent structure, given the importance of the Community, and as a memorial to its founder, Cardinal Newman. At first, the building of the new church wasn't without controversy, but

---

1. 'John Ronald Reuel Tolkien (1892-1973)' *The Oratory Parish Magazine*, May 1909, *Birmingham Oratory*, <http://www.birminghamoratory.org.uk/about-the-oratory/tolkien-the-oratory> [accessed 12 December 2017].
2. As proof of his closeness to the Oratory's daily life, it is worth pointing out that he possessed a Latin dictionary, found by chance in 2016 at the Liverpool Hope University, which previously belonged to Fr. Ignatius Ryder, who died in 1907. He had been the second provost of the Oratory elected after the death of Cardinal Newman.
3. Humphrey Carpenter, (ed.), *The Letters of J.R.R. Tolkien*, Houghton Mifflin, Boston, 1981, Letter 306, p. 395.
4. Op. cit.

eventually it was successfully carried out. The construction was planned in a remarkable way, as the structure of the new church was built around the old edifice, so that the original chapel could remain in use for much of the time during the works. The new church was opened in 1906, although the works were completed in 1909, coinciding with the Golden Jubilee of the Oratory School and the anniversary of John Henry Newman's promotion to cardinal.

Several beautifully decorated confessionals were acquired for the new church, each of them manufactured in a different country: namely Spain, Italy, Germany, Belgium and England. How could it have been otherwise? Morgan was responsible for the Spanish confessional and there he exercised his sacramental tasks for many years. At that time, confessions were in higher demand than at present, which meant that these could take up extended periods of time. It should also be noted that only priests with the relevant knowledge and theological formation could perform this task (in fact, not all members of the Community were able to do so), which proves that Francis Morgan's intellectual preparation wasn't at all negligible.

The priest's daily life, once he had assumed guardianship of the Tolkiens, experienced a few changes. His room, which was already generally busy, became even more so as Morgan's books, many of which were in Spanish, became a powerful attraction for his wards, especially the eldest. The foreign language, instead of serving as an obstacle, actually helped Ronald develop a remarkable delight for Spanish:

> Spanish was another [language which gave to Tolkien linguistic-aesthetic satisfaction]: my guardian was half Spanish, and in my early teens I used to pinch his books and try to learn it: the only Romance language that gives me the particular pleasure of which I am speaking-it.[5]

Priscilla Tolkien confirms this fact and argues that:

> My father's great interest in the Spanish language must have been due to a large extent because of his close connection with Father Francis.[6]

Tolkien's interest in this language was alive[7] throughout the years.[8] In 1967, he replied to an offer to translate *The Lord of the Rings* into Spanish

---

5. Op. cit. [3], Letter 163, p. 213.
6. From the author's correspondence with Priscilla Tolkien.
7. Thereafter the prominence of this work mainly fell on John *Ronald* Reuel Tolkien, who would of course eventually become a famous author. Therefore, references to "Tolkien" from now shall refer to him and not his brother, unless Hilary is explicitly named.
8. In fact, when, in the mid-sixties, he received a copy of the first translation of his works into Spanish, an Argentinian edition of *The Hobbit*, he wrote a dedication in it to his wife in Spanish: "*Para Edita querida*" ("To dear Edith"). This book was given as a gift to a Spanish priest named Antonio Quevedo who, in 1973, supported Fr. John Tolkien, Tolkien's eldest son, when his father died.

from a Canadian priest living in Spain, called David L. Sands, and said:

> I have some acquaintance with the Spanish language on both sides of the Atlantic and I find it, especially the European variety, extremely attractive.[9]

Tolkien was fond of inventing languages from an early age and, although Morgan never taught him Spanish, he found in it a starting point for the creation of an imaginary language: *Naffarin*. Little is known about it, except what Tolkien himself explained in a 1931 essay about his hobby of conceiving private languages, entitled *A Secret Vice*.

Only a poem of four lines, constituting a single sentence, remains from *Naffarin*:

> O Naffarínos cutá vu navru cangor
> luttos ca vúna tiéranar,
> dana maga tíer ce vru encá vún' farta
> once ya merúta vúna maxt' amámen.

There have been many attempts to translate these words, and even to relate them to the Elvish languages developed years later by Tolkien. Among these attempts, Christopher Gilson[10] excels. Gilson, speculating about the Spanish and Latin origins of this language, presented a plausible translation:[11]

> O Naffarines recite forever poetry composed here in your own land that great land, which ever you call home and now deserves your increased love.

Going back to Fr. Morgan's book collection, it was unfortunately scattered many years ago, although some of them occasionally reappear in the most surprising places.[12] They are easily identifiable by their bookplate, featuring Morgan's personal coat of arms with his motto, his Latin name (*Franciscus Morgan et Osborne*), and an indication of his Oratorian congregation.

A deer and a griffin are represented above this coat of arms, formed by

---

9. Eduardo Segura. "Spanish Language" in Michael Drout (ed.), *The J. R. R. Tolkien Encyclopedia: Scholarship and Critical Assessment*, Routledge, New York, 2006, p. 624.
10. Christopher Gilson is a member of the Elvish Linguistic Fellowship (an international organisation devoted to the scholarly study of the invented languages of J.R.R. Tolkien) and the chief editor of the journal *Parma Eldalamberon*, dedicated to this subject.
11. His detailed reasoning is only available, as far as I know, in a post published in a specialised mailing list, and available in <https://groups.yahoo.com/neo/groups/%20lambengolmor/conversations/topics/492> [accessed 12 December 2017].
12. As mentioned above, Morgan's books have been lost, mixed, destroyed or sold for charity. However, in 2011 a young Australian named Robert Hiini announced the discovery of one of these books in the bargain bin of an antique shop in Rockingham, a city in Western Australia, south-west of Perth (more than 9,000 miles from Birmingham). It is *Nova et Vetera* from George Tyrrell and, besides featuring his bookplate, was personally signed by Francis Morgan and dated 1907.

the union of two shields. The right one represents the Morgan branch of the family, with a griffin segreant sable, and the left one the Osborne branch. This features a cross which divides it into four rectangular zones (first and fourth decorated and second and third in blank). This is one of the variants of the family crest for this surname; in Spain, they used a different one. The motto is a quote from the Roman poet Ovid: "UT AMERIS AMABILIS ESTO"; that is "To be loved, be lovable", which was certainly an explicit statement of Francis' principles.

As for the themes and genres of Morgan's book collection, aside from the religious ones, he would surely have had some written by his illustrious ancestors. If we take into account the influence of his great grandfather, Juan Nicolás Böhl de Faber, he probably also would have had some classics of Spanish literature, most likely from the *Spanish Golden Age*.

In any case, the young Tolkien would have been familiar with Spanish culture. In addition to what he could learn from his guardian's books, he plied Morgan for facts about Spain,[13] which certainly must have served as entertainment for many evenings. As such, it opens an interesting line of speculation about a possible influence on Tolkien's work and can be ventured that it served as inspiration for some of the passages and scenes from his future writings.

Beyond this, which is to some extent anecdotal, something that should be intellectually stressed from this formative period of Tolkien's life, while he was a ward of Fr. Morgan, is the development of his own religious vision. It was clearly inspired by the erudition he received while in contact with the Oratory and also by the circumstances of that time.

Those years coincided with the momentous pontificate of Pope Pius X (1903 - 1914), a crucial period for the Catholic Church, as it defined its position in direct opposition to the growing secular spirit of the society of that time. Pius X explained his view of "theological modernism" in his encyclical *Lamentabili and Pascendi dominici Gregis* (1907). He stated that to follow or implement agnostic, immanentist or evolutionist reinterpretations of the Catholic doctrine was an attack on faith and, therefore, against the foundations of the Church.

Tolkien, reflecting on this some years later, said:

> I suppose the greatest reform of our time was that carried out by St Pius X: surpassing anything, however needed, that the [Second Vatican] Council will achieve.[14]

---

13. Daniel Grotta, *J.R.R. Tolkien: Architect of Middle-Earth*, Running Press, Philadelphia, 1976, p. 74.
14. Op. cit. [3], Letter 250, p. 339. Carpenter interprets "the greatest reform of our time" as a possible allusion to Pius X's recommendation of daily communion and children's communion. However, Tolkien could also have been referring to all actions urged by the Pope against modernism and its possible danger in relation to philosophy, apologetics, exegesis, history, liturgy and discipline.

Some critics stress the similarity between the spirit of Pius X and the moral foundations that permeate Tolkien's stories. Thus, A.R. Bossert wrote:

> An intellectually sophisticated and orthodox Catholic, Tolkien also exhibited awareness of early twentieth-century Church policies later in his life. *The Silmarillion*, *The Hobbit*, and *The Lord of the Rings* all parallel the anti-modernist rhetoric of *Pascendi dominici gregis* in their assertion of truth in ancient stories, suspicion of historical criticism with its glamour of intellectualism, and their condemnation of a tool that is too dangerous to be used.[15]

Although there had been some initial controversy about harmony between the concepts expressed by the Pope and the thinking of Cardinal Newman, which Pius X strove to clarify[16], it is more than likely that Pius X's ideas were emphasised through Tolkien by additional factors. There was a prominent figure in the Oratory, whose close relationship with the Vatican authorities would likely have enhanced the impact of Pius X's pastoral message among those linked to it: Fr. Denis Sheil, the closest friend, correspondent and confidant of the influential Cardinal Merry del Val, Vatican secretary of state and Pius X's right-hand man.

Denis Sheil is the same priest named in Tolkien's coded letter from the summer of 1904, wherein he simply refers to him as Fr. Denis. Born in Dublin in 1865, the youngest son of General Sir Justin Sheil, the British Minister to Persia, Sheil had attended the Oratory School, as had his older brothers, and returned there in 1890 to begin his novitiate after completing his studies and being ordained in Rome. Among his classmates at the Pontifical Scots College in Rome was the future Cardinal Merry del Val, who was about the same age as him, and the two developed a deep friendship. In addition, they were distant relatives, as one of Fr. Denis' sisters was the Cardinal's aunt.

It seems that Morgan wasn't oblivious of this matter, as the Community was small and it was a theologically relevant issue.[17] On the other hand, it is likely that he also had contact with Cardinal Merry del Val: both were Anglo-Spaniards and their families frequented the same circles; the Cardinal's father was secretary to the Spanish legation in London; his mother, Sofia de Zulueta, was from an ennobled family of Basque origin (the Counts of

---

15. A. R. Bossert, ""Surely You Don't Disbelieve": Tolkien and Pius X: Anti-Modernism in Middle-earth." *Mythlore* 25:1-2 (Autumn-Winter 2006), p. 53.
16. The Provost of the Oratory, Father John Norris, wrote a letter to the Times of London on November 4th 1907 stating that the "highest authority" told them that the doctrine and the spirit of the Catholic teachings of Newman did not come into conflict with the Papal Encyclical and also that the only censurable thing were the ideas of those who mistakenly sought refuge behind a great name. These criticisms could be applicable, for example, to one of the most prominent modernist theologians of that period, the Jesuit George Tyrrell, who inspired by the ideas of Cardinal Newman converted to Catholicism, but was finally excommunicated in 1907 because of his declared differences with Pius X.
17. Curiously, the book found in Australia from the Morgan's collection was written by George Tyrrell.

Torre Díaz), who established their business offices in Cadiz and London in the early 19th century.[18]

Aside from these issues, since he had taken on the responsibility of caring for the Tolkien brothers, Fr. Morgan used to often travel with them and they would take vacations together. The visits to Rednal continued, and sometimes the three of them went to the retreat for priests, where the boys could escape to the countryside and re-live, even if for a short time, moments from their past. Ronald would later go to Rednal to prepare for the exams that won him a scholarship at Oxford.

According to Daniel Grotta (one of Tolkien's biographers)[19], shortly after the death of Mabel Tolkien, Morgan took the children on a fifteen-day holiday to Wales. This aroused a deep passion for the Welsh language in Ronald, which employed unusual spellings, as he was able to see on the signs in the train stations. It seems that, in fact, Tolkien had discovered the Welsh language long before, while living with his mother in King's Heath, near a station where trains with coal from Wales usually arrived. For the purposes of this book, the existence of this trip indicates Morgan's relationship with his Welsh background though, unfortunately, it isn't known if the purpose of the trip was purely for pleasure or for some other reason.

The trips that have been officially documented are those made over the course of several summers by Morgan and his wards to the south coast of England; in particular to Lyme Regis in Dorset. Morgan liked this place and spent many of their summer holidays there, when he didn't travel to Spain.[20] The environment and landscapes of Lyme Regis are certainly spectacular. The author Deborah Cadbury describes them:

> The cliffs tower over the surrounding landscape. The town hugs the coast under the lee of a hill that protects it from the south-westerly wind. To the west, the harbour is sheltered by the Cobb, a long, curling sea wall stretching out into the English Channel – the waves breaking ceaselessly along its perimeter. To the east, the boundary of the local graveyard clings to the disintegrating Church Cliffs, with lichen-covered gravestones jutting out to the sky at awkward angles. Beyond this runs the dark, forbidding crag face of Black Ven, damp from sea spray.[21]

---

18. Besides being bankers and carrying out commercial exports activities, another one of its business segments were related to shipping companies so that, for example, in 1840 they obtained the maritime concession of the first ferry line between Cadiz and Port St Mary. Also the Cardinal's grandfather married the daughter of the founder of the shipping company P&O and the run of this business also remained in the family.

19. In general terms, Grotta's work can be described as deeply flawed, but he was the first Tolkien's biographer and, unlike many others later, he was able to meet people who firsthand witnesses his life.

20. Morgan's link with south west England is remarkable. Firstly, his family by his maternal grandfather came from Paignton (Devon) and, on the other hand, it is known that he visited Lynton (Devon) at least in 1890 and Lyme Regis (Dorset) repeatedly.

21. Deborah Cadbury, *The Dinosaur Hunters: A True Story of Scientific Rivalry and the Discovery of the*

Lyme Regis is a well-known place for finding fossils and prehistoric remains. One of its most famous daughters is Anne Manning, who lived there in the 19th century and who discovered various creatures from the distant past of our planet.

The three travellers stayed at The Three Cups Hotel on Broad Street, the city's main street. There, in 1906, at fourteen years old, Tolkien sketched a picture of the Cobb and entitled it "Lyme Regis Harbour from the Drawing Room of The Three Cups Hotel". They were able to take part in various different activities when staying there. For instance, they could take walks along the coast or visit areas surrounding the town. After the 1908 landslide, after which many fossils were uncovered, the Tolkien brothers found a large fossilised bone and the romantically-minded Ronald thought that it was a petrified dragon bone.[22]

Another type of distraction that Morgan enjoyed was visiting acquaintances in the area, such as the Mathews. They were an important family of Irish origin who Morgan had developed a friendship with through the head of the family, Francis James Mathew. He was a lawyer and a novelist, married to Agnes Elizabeth Ann, daughter of the prominent politician James Tisdall Woodroffe, who attended the Birmingham Oratory school with his cousins, Theobald and Charles James. The three cousins were great-nephews of the famous *Apostle of Temperance*, Theobald Mathew.[23]

The Mathews had two children who, years later, would take up positions in the Catholic Church. The eldest brother, David, born in 1902, would become Archbishop. Gervase, who was born three years later, was a Dominican priest who exercised his mission in Oxford, where he was also a lecturer at Blackfriars. He developed a deep friendship with Tolkien. In fact, he is considered a member of *The Inklings*, Tolkien's literary circle.

An appealing aspect of these trips was the chance to spend a few days away from the bustle of the big city and to simply enjoy each other's company. Morgan treated the Tolkien brothers as if they were his own children and cared deeply about their problems, to the extent that he had a good understanding of them. During the holidays of 1908, thanks to his insightful nature, he realised the boys weren't happy living with their aunt Beatrice, although they didn't formally complain about her. It was clear that he would have to find other accommodation for them.

Shortly after returning from holiday, they moved in with the Faulkners, neighbors of the Oratory, who rented out the rooms of their family home. The benefits of the change were immediately evident, as the boys' mood

---

Prehistoric World, HarperCollins, London, 2001, p. 3.
22. Humphrey Carpenter, *J.R.R Tolkien: A biography*, George Allen & Unwin, London, 1977, p. 38.
23. Theobald Mathew (1790-1856). Irish Capuchin priest. Concerned by Irish social problems, he led the abstinence movement, with great effect in Ireland, the United Kingdom and United States. He became a real celebrity in his time.

significantly improved.

However, as we shall see, this move would also cause other difficulties.

A Rainy Day (A Day in the Life)

Edgbaston, 1908.

It was hard to explain why, after so many years, rainy days like this brought upon him a nagging sense of unease and deep melancholy. The curious thing is that it didn't always happen. On the contrary, they usually passed without him noticing them.

The day had begun as usual with the morning Mass, assisted by one of the Tolkien brothers. Today it was Hilary's turn, the youngest. He was very happy with the boys. The Holy Spirit had entrusted him with a complex mission, but contact with these children, who would soon be men, was a blessing. Indeed, it came with many responsibilities, but they were great boys and, on the other hand, this duty was extremely important. He knew he had to do his best as their guardian.

His own father had taken on a similar mission when his grandfather had died, but the situation was completely different then. His uncles Tomás and Juanito were older than the Tolkiens, and his father's duty had been mainly related to the business. Plus, grandmother Aurora had still been alive, whereas the Tolkiens were all alone.

He was pleased with the move he had arranged. Their aunt hadn't given them the love they needed. Perhaps this was because she had been recently widowed, or maybe it was because of the longstanding antipathy between Protestants and Catholics (which even affected those from the same family, but followed different religions). The truth is that the appearance and character of the boys had improved greatly since they had begun staying with Mrs Faulkner.

It also brought him relief. Dealing with someone who requested four pounds and sixteen shillings every month just to take care of her own nephews was hard. It was different with Mrs Faulkner though, who was ultimately a stranger who merely rented out rooms. Paradoxically though, they were much happier at her home than with their aunt.

Today, he wouldn't see them until the evening. He wanted to discuss their savings, but he was sure they wouldn't pay much attention. They trusted him blindly and, though they would listen to him respectfully, they were more concerned about what happened at school than about their income. The eldest, Ronald, only seemed to care about rugby, but he did have enormous talent and seemed destined for great things - an extremely hard task, being a Catholic, and an orphan with limited resources. However, it was his responsibility to help Ronald achieve his goals. He knew so many people whose lives were wasted...

But now it was time to take care of other matters and stop thinking about the boys for a while. This year had been particularly overwhelming, with everyone rushing around. Work on the new church would be completed next year, coinciding with the Golden Jubilee of the School and the thirtieth anniversary of "the Father" becoming cardinal. If he had been alive to see this, how happy he would have been! The new church was magnificent.

Blessed rain! He had several visits to make. The Villanuevas were waiting for him to make preparations for their child's christening. They were an agreeable couple, also of Spanish origin, although their grandfather had come to England for different reasons than his own. Fr. Denis had overseen their marriage three years ago, and they usually attended Sunday Mass. After that, he would have to visit other houses in the neighbourhood, but he didn't want to stray too far. His legs weren't as strong as they once had been and, at present, with the increase in traffic, it was dangerous going out into the streets on rainy days.

Times changed. He still remembered the image of Hagley Road when he had seen it for the first time. How different it all had been! No cars, or electricity... Time quietly altered the places where life ran its course, and minor differences seemed imperceptible until a day like this, when one realised just how much everything had really changed.

It wasn't only places that had been transformed; people too. Generations passed, and natural law inexorably filled the gaps. Some passed on to a better place and others, like him, simply grew older, little by little, leaving behind, as if it were another life, so many special moments. However, some memories refused to disappear, so it was hard for him to forget the bewilderment which had invaded his childhood mind when he had realised how different the big English cities were from Port St Mary. And yet, he had become just one more of its inhabitants and almost all of his life had passed there.

But enough of daydreams! This wasn't the place, or the time, for it. There were many things to do, and he wasn't in Rednal; this wasn't an idle period – besides, these reflections were more typical of someone like Fr. Joseph. The best thing he could do was to thank God that no misfortune had come to them when the chimney stack had fallen. How fortunate was Fr. John that he hadn't been in his room, and Fr. Henry, whose guardian angel had protected him when the chimney had crashed down, carrying him with it from his room on the top floor to the parish library on the ground floor. Certainly, that would be difficult to forget.

Tasks called to him from every direction and he had to carry them out right away, or he would never be able to finish them all. Everybody else was already at work. The rain couldn't keep him any longer. Ultimately, he was in England, where beautiful weather was unusual.

Tonight, he should write home.

The Love Affair

It was 1908 when the Tolkien brothers moved into the Faulkner's house. The family was comprised of the father, Louis, who was just over sixty years old, his wife Louisa Elizabeth, in her mid-fifties, and their daughter Helen, an unmarried woman in her early thirties. Before this, Louis Faulkner had run a business in London, with Robert Hankinson Cox, called Faulkner & Co., Continental Carriers, Custom House Agents and Ship-owners.[1] Their head office was at 61 Great Tower Street, very close to the Morgan Brothers headquarters, and its activities were related to the transport of wine and spirits, among other products. It is therefore very likely that Fr. Morgan already knew them beyond the fact that they lived near the Oratory, in their house at 37 Duchess Road, in Edgbaston.

In this new home, the boys faced many new situations. Focusing on Ronald Tolkien, who was at that time sixteen years old, one of his main concerns was the approaching end of his school years at King Edward's, and the long-awaited, albeit uncertain, possibility of continuing his studies at university. Hilary's case was different as, unlike his older brother, he didn't appear to be interested in higher education. In addition, Ronald's educational achievements were remarkable, as they had been since childhood. This was a fact that was clear to many of his teachers and, of course, to his close relations.

Certain episodes had enriched him both personally and intellectually. The misfortunes of his childhood had strengthened him, though they had left a residue of grief in him. Possibly because of the influence of his guardian, this trauma was barely noticeable in Tolkien. He had a strong, nonconformist temperament, reinforced by his confidence where religious was concerned.

Nevertheless, at sixteen he was in a difficult period of life, between childhood and adulthood. A new world loomed in the near future, with the possibility of achieving long-coveted goals, while trying to overcome serious obstacles. His first and main problem was an economic one. His mother hadn't left enough inheritance to cover the costs of a university education and, although Fr. Morgan was willing to help him with some of the tuition fees, he needed to win a scholarship if he was to access higher education. This was an enormously difficult challenge which he would need

---

1. Humphrey Carpenter, Tolkien's official biographer, incorrectly described Faulkner as a wine merchant. This mistake was probably derived from his possible relationship with Morgan and his family's background in this area.

to devote all of his energies to.

He wanted to attend Oxford University, though none of his relations had studied there, as opposed to Morgan's. Suffice it to say, several Osbornes attended Oxford (they were of the branch of the family that didn't emigrate to Spain). The last of these was his great uncle Peter who, over half a century before, had graduated from Exeter College (the same college that Tolkien would eventually attend). Under different historical circumstances, it is quite likely that Francis Morgan would have also studied at Oxford. He was unable to do so because of the self-imposed Catholic ban, which lasted until late into the 19th century, from attending Oxford. This was in spite of opposition from many Catholics, even notable personalities from the Church, such as Cardinal Newman.

There was an implicit pact between Tolkien and Fr. Francis whereby, if the young man wanted to enter Oxford, after winning a scholarship, the priest would pay all remaining expenses (which were significant at the time). It was not a trivial agreement, and Tolkien was keen to accept it. But then, something unexpected happened.

When the boys began living as guests of the Faulkners, their quality of life improved, given that they were treated better than they had been at their aunt's house. What's more, because they lived so close to the Oratory, their daily life continued normally, with everything following a stable routine, their time divided between school life and the Oratory's activities. However, a young girl, who was also staying at the Faulkner house, crossed Ronald's path. This girl was Edith Bratt. She was also an orphan, but not a Catholic, and was older than him, at nineteen years of age.

A friendship soon flourished between them, which transformed into love; young and somewhat idealised, but love nonetheless. Right from the beginning of their relationship, Tolkien surely had to know how inappropriate it was. It was a powerful distraction from his academic entry tests for Oxford, for one thing. There were other issues too, though still important, such as the age gap (she was three years older than him and this was not exactly the norm in those days), and then there was the difference in religious creeds.

These circumstances explain why they kept their relationship secret, or rather, why they tried to be as cautious as possible. In the guesthouse, nobody knew about it; likewise in school and, of course, Morgan was completely oblivious to what was happening. However, during an innocent bike ride to Rednal, they were spotted by the doorkeeper of the Oratory retreat, who was an acquaintance of Mrs Church, and she reported this to her. She also mentioned it to the Oratory's cook, through whom the story finally made its way to the ears of Fr. Morgan.

Although their tender love story was completely free of malice, it caused several problems. On the one hand, Tolkien had betrayed his guardian's trust by hiding significant facts from him (probably guessing what his reaction would be). His actions could also have been interpreted as irresponsible, given that he was devoting his time to something outside of his immediate priority (his education), especially given the proximity of the scholarship exams. Finally, it could have been viewed as a deliberate attempt to lie and deceive everyone who had trusted and helped him with all means at their disposal.

Accordingly, Fr. Morgan's reaction was strong. For the first time, at least in reaction to an important issue, he imposed his authority over Ronald. Using his power as legal guardian, he forbade him to have any contact with Edith while he was his ward; that is, until Tolkien reached the age of majority. At the same time, he moved the Tolkien brothers to the McSherry household, a Catholic family who also lived near the Oratory.

Morgan's attitude has been extensively discussed, but few have understood the reasons for his firmness. Yet the truth is that he has been judged through the lens of a different period and perspective, so his actions have been distorted. He is often painted as an uncompromising, jealous, tyrannical and severe guardian. Some authors even dare to venture the outlandish notion that Morgan reacted as he did because the love affair would crush his secret hope of Tolkien becoming a Catholic priest. This idea is somewhat absurd and certainly inconsistent with many of his past actions, such as that of allowing Tolkien to attend King Edward's.

Strictly speaking, none of these judgments correspond to reality. After all, we have to appreciate the context of the early 20th century, when appearances were everything and issues which are currently trivial were, at that time, fundamental. Rightly or wrongly, Morgan was acting as a father, and so he put the future of his ward ahead of what seemed to him to be momentary happiness. The benefits of Tolkien gaining entry to Oxford University and being able to carve out his own future seemed the greater consideration.

Tolkien didn't have adequate resources to provide for himself, or practical training for gaining any kind of employment. Moreover, being Catholic was still an important social disadvantage, so if he had abandoned everything to be with Edith at that time, his life would probably have been condemned to misfortune. As such, he resigned himself to accepting his guardian's decision. In any case, it would have been difficult to disobey him, given that Tolkien was so dependent on him both financially and legally. However, it's also likely that his decision to honour Morgan's decree had as much to do with Tolkien's intense feelings of affection and gratitude towards him. Years later, he reflected on this:

I had to choose between disobeying and grieving (or deceiving) a guardian who had been a father to me, more than most real fathers, but without any obligation, and "dropping" the love-affair until I was 21. I don't regret my decision, though it was very hard on my lover.[2]

Thus, although Tolkien's obedience wasn't absolute (there were a few liaisons, both coincidental and planned, which greatly angered Fr. Morgan), contact between Ronald and Edith eased off. Eventually, she moved to Cheltenham to live with relatives.

Tolkien earned his scholarship for Oxford, after one failed attempt, and enrolled at Exeter College in 1911. That summer, he made a trip to Switzerland with his brother, who was working on a farm in Sussex. Joining Oxford brought with it a separation from his guardian for an extended period, for the first time in many years.

Despite Tolkien's love affair with Edith Bratt causing a temporary deterioration in his relationship with Morgan, the Oratory remained Tolkien's refuge and he returned there whenever he could. In fact, it remained his permanent address for a long time, as can be seen, for example, in his Army documents.

During Tolkien's early years in Oxford, the memory of his relationship with Edith continued to live on in his heart. Perhaps because of their separation, the bond between them grew stronger, while time and distance helped them to mature. Some authors think (and even Tolkien says something to this effect)[3] that Morgan's firmness turned what was possibly temporary young love into a deep relationship. So, when Tolkien turned twenty-one, at exactly twelve o'clock on his birthday[4], he began a long letter to Edith (he hadn't been in touch with her in three years). Their relationship was soon rekindled and, after a brief period, due to him going off to fight in the Great War, they were joined in marriage.

Morgan accepted all of this without opposition. John and Priscilla Tolkien (two of Tolkien's children) recall their parents telling them about how, when Tolkien was an Oxford student, Morgan would occasionally travel by train from Birmingham to visit, sometimes accompanied by Edith. During these trips, Morgan sometimes demonstrated his own particular personality. For example, during one of these journeys, he was determined to get off at Banbury, one of the stops along the way, to buy Banbury Cakes. These were flat, greasy pastry cakes, typical of the town.[5]

When Tolkien and Edith first got back together, his academic career

---

2. Humphrey Carpenter, (ed.), *The Letters of J.R.R. Tolkien*, Houghton Mifflin, Boston, 1981, Letter 43, p. 53.
3. Op. cit.
4. Humphrey Carpenter, *J.R.R Tolkien: A biography*, George Allen & Unwin, London, 1977, p. 60.
5. John and Priscilla Tolkien, *The Tolkien Family Album*, Houghton Mifflin, Boston, 1992, p. 35.

suffered a little. Thankfully, his attitude soon changed and he began to flourish. He also got a job during the summer of 1913, which indicates how he was doing his best to succeed. The job was acting as a preceptor, accompanying three young upper-class Mexicans during a trip to France to visit their aunts, who lived there. The boys, who were studying in England, were Ventura, José and Eustaquio Martínez Río y Bermejillo. They belonged to one of the most important and wealthy Mexican families, who also had roots and close ties to Spain. Unfortunately, the trip was marked by the accidental death of one of the aunts and became a bitter personal experience for Tolkien.

What should be noted is that this was his first serious job, and it is quite likely that he needed the help of Morgan and his contacts to get it. Despite an apparent connection between Tolkien and a cousin of the boys who was studying at Oxford (and who years later became the illustrious historian, Pablo Martínez del Río y Vinent), there was also a coincidental relationship between the Martínez del Río y Bermejillo family and Morgan. This, at the very least, surely enhanced the credentials of an inexperienced young man like Tolkien. The link between this family and Morgan lies with Catalina des Fontaines y Barron, an intimate friend of his mother. Catalina was a close relative of Eustace (Eustaquio) and William (Guillermo) Barron, who were established merchants in Mexico. They had close ties, through both business and family, with the Bermejillos (the maternal branch of the boys' family). In fact, it's likely that Eustaquio was named after Eustace Barron.

Looking back at this period and beyond these facts, the proof of how much Father Francis Morgan meant to Tolkien can be found in his secret passion: the creation of languages. In 1917, during the war, the future author was beginning to formulate the works that would lead him to fame. One of the first steps was the creation of the proto-languages which were the precursors to his Elvish languages. Two of his first attempts were *Gnomish* and *Qenya*. In the Gnomish Lexicon[6] there is a curious entry:

Faidron o **Faithron** = Francis

In fact, it is an unquestionable statement of respect and deep admiration for his guardian, because those words are variations of a proper name (only proper names are capitalised in the Gnomish Lexicon) and the sign = is used to match names in different languages.

This kind of license was common in the early development period of

---

6. The *Gnomish Lexicon* was published in the journal *Parma Eldalamberon* as "The Grammar and Lexicon of the GNOMISH TONGUE, by J. R. R. Tolkien", Christopher Gilson, Carl F. Hostetter, Patrick Wynne and Arden R. Smith (eds.), *Parma Eldalamberon* 11 (1995), p. 33.

Tolkien's fictional universe, and the appearance of *Francis* in the Gnomish Lexicon isn't as unusual as it might seem. In several contemporary manuscripts, there are characters who correspond with real people from his family. For example, Lirillo or Noldorin, Amillo and Erinti, which are representations of Ronald, Hilary and Edith respectively, all make appearances in the Qenya Lexicon. What is remarkable is that the meanings of these Elvish names usually contain significant metaphors. In the case of *Faidron* and *Faithron*, there is a clear connection with the entries which appear next to them in the Gnomish Lexicon:

> **fair** free, unconstrained
> **faidwen** freedom
> **faith** liberty
> **faithir** liberator, Saviour

Linking Francis with these indicates that Tolkien felt no resentment towards him. What's more, it's telling that, in his private world, within his personal creation, he composed the name of his guardian using roots related to "liberty" or "liberator". This is probably more valuable than any explicit statement, and stresses the importance of Francis Morgan in his life; he helped Tolkien when his mother died, *liberated* him from the relatives who wanted him to give up Catholicism, and accompanied him on this path throughout his life.

The Great War

World War One can be described as one of the cruellest conflicts in history. From its onset, which at the time suggested a quick outcome, all calculations on its development proved to be wrong and that no one really understood the consequences of a global war with the level of military technology at that time. Nobody foresaw, even remotely, the devastating effects of the modern weapons or, for example, the important role to be played by aviation.

It was a dirty war, without limits, and with no real understanding of how far the human desire for destruction could go. It led many young people, inspired in many cases by a naive idealism, to devote themselves to it with passion. They succumbed to the ceaseless bloodletting, often justifying it using clichés about honour and justice, which rather hid the real disaster of an obsolete military strategy. A whole generation of Englishmen was affected by the war and many of its finest youth of that time gave their lives fighting in the trenches.

The war began in August 1914, surprising Francis Morgan in Spain. After several years of absence, due to the attention he had been paying to his wards during his holiday periods, he returned to Spain consecutively every summer from 1911 to 1914. In 1911, the Tolkien brothers took their own path: the eldest began his studies at Oxford, and the younger went to work in Sussex. In this way, some of Morgan's obligations were reduced.

Nevertheless, there was a significant family reason which justified his trip to Spain in 1914. On July 25th, his young cousin Antonio Osborne Guezala, son of his late uncle Tomás Osborne Böhl de Faber, was ordained a priest and entered into the Society of Jesus. In August, he celebrated his first Mass at the church of San Francisco in Port St Mary. According to the *Revista Portuense*, "Francisco Morgan y Osborne, Oratorian religious" was the master of ceremonies at this Mass, which the new priest concelebrated with other members of the Society of Jesus. There was a banquet hosted by the Count of Osborne (brother of Antonio) and the three Morgan brothers were invited, as members of the family. It is noteworthy that this news made the cover of the local newspaper, alongside the bombing of Belgrade, which was one of the first military actions at the beginning of the war.

His return to England after this surely must have been an adventure for the mature Fr. Francis, since Great Britain's entry into the conflict (on August 4th, when Germany invaded Belgium) was causing difficulties for journeys by sea for British subjects. There is no evidence of him returning to Spain during the war, unlike his brother Augusto, who at that time resided in Portugal and was able to travel by land.

There were deaths in most families, even amongst those at the Oratory, which lost several of its older school boys. Many of the former students had chosen a military career, so were the first to be mobilised. Some were veterans who had fought in other conflicts, such as the Anglo-Boer War, and had reached a high military rank, but the younger ones were subalterns, and many of them suffered a terrible fate.

The first to fall was Captain Fergus Forbes of the Royal Irish Regiment, just twenty days after the start of the war. After him, another eighty-three former students from the Oratory School lost their lives. These first deaths caused great sadness to fall on the Oratory, increasing the deeply personal concerns of community members who had someone close to them fighting on the front. Fr. Edward Pereira, for instance, had two brothers in the military, George and Cecil, both former students of the Oratory. They were at constant risk throughout the four years of the war.

From Morgan's direct circle, he lost several relatives[1], but also acquaintances, neighbours and parishioners. Names like Somme, Verdun and Ypress became synonymous with death.

In the first months of the war, a large number of civilians throughout the United Kingdom voluntarily enrolled. In particular, the Birmingham area was one of the greatest points of recruitment so that, in the course of one month, there were three Pals Battalions formed from the inhabitants of the city. Members of these battalions were men from the same area, joining the army together, so they were fighting alongside neighbours and friends, which was good for morale and coexistence.

Hilary Tolkien enlisted in one of these regiments in October, joining the Third Battalion of Birmingham, the redesigned 16th Royal Warwicks. He enlisted as a bugler and was trained at Moseley School, which had become a training centre. After three moves across England, his battalion was finally sent to the front on November 21th 1915. During the fighting, Hilary served in the medical corps as a stretcher bearer, and he was wounded in April 1916.

His brother Ronald, eager to complete his studies, joined the Officer Training Corps at Oxford and thus deferred his enlistment until he obtained his degree in mid-1915. He was commissioned as a Second Lieutenant in the Lancashire Fusiliers and was sent abroad to France in June 1916, where he was transferred to the 11th Battalion.

---

1. His cousin, Major Cecil Buckley Morgan, the son of his uncle Thomas, fell in France, along with his son Basil. Also, Roland Morgan, the only son of Aaron Herbert Morgan (brother of Cecil and former partner of Morgan Brothers Ltd), served in the Royal Flying Corps and died on the Western Front.

However, before his move to the continent, several important events happened in his life. His romance with Edith Bratt had resumed after three years of separation, with the ultimate goal of marriage. One of the key focusses was her conversion to Catholicism, an essential step for their union. It meant she had to move to a rented house in the city of Warwick, as the relatives providing her with accommodation were opposed to the relationship.

Given Tolkien's move to the frontline of the war and his wedding day were both imminent, he went to discuss economic issues with Fr. Morgan. However, perhaps feeling uneasy about reigniting Morgan's past objections to his relationship with Edith, Tolkien decided not to mention their planned marriage.

Thus, Morgan knew nothing of his ward's plans until fifteen days before the wedding, when he received a letter from Tolkien revealing the event. Despite this, his response was warm, and he wished them happiness and bestowed his blessings. He also suggested that the ceremony be held at the Oratory, but arrangements had already been made and they were married on March 22th 1916, in the Catholic church in Warwick.

In June 1916, Tolkien was informed that he had to leave for the front and he decided to spend his last night with his young wife in the Plough and Harrow Hotel in Birmingham, just around the corner from the Oratory. In a situation of such anguish and with an uncertain future ahead, it was probably a big relief to be there; Morgan, who had cared for him since childhood, would be able to see him off with words of consolation.

Shortly after arriving on the continent, Tolkien serves as a communications officer at the Battle of the Somme, which was one of the deadliest conflicts of the war. Fortunately, he wasn't seriously injured there, but contracted "trench fever" and, in November 1916, he was sent back to England to recover. It's fair to say that he was very fortunate, because the war was fierce and the casualties were countless. In fact, from among his group of closest friends, only Christopher Wiseman survived.

The progress of the war led to a situation of global mobilisation. This also affected the Fathers of the Oratory, and some of them went to the front as military chaplains. Among them, to cite just a few, were Fr. Anthony Pollen, who was over fifty years old at the time. He served in the Navy as a warship chaplain, and was wounded and widely honoured during the naval Battle of Jutland. There was also Fr. Stanislaus du Moulin-Browne; he went on to be highly decorated, as part of the 1st Battalion of the Irish Guards, and played a big role after the armistice with the German prisoners, given his linguistic knowledge.

Among such death and destruction, one event in late 1917 compensated for Tolkien's recent suffering. Still convalescent, and not yet officially discharged from the army, Ronald reported to Morgan that his first child had been born at Cheltenham. The priest travelled there to officiate at the baptism of the newborn, who was named John Francis Reuel. The child's second given name, Francis, is of course significant in this context.

The war finally ended in 1918. Almost all who participated in it, including the priests of the Oratory, needed a long time to recover from the deep mental and physical wounds that the conflict had caused. Nothing was ever the same again; the world, it seemed, had lost its innocence.

As with every war, there were heroes and victims. Adrian Carton de Wiart, an old boy of the Oratory, stood out among the heroes and was one of the most decorated members of the British Army. Others, like Major Hubert Galton[2], another old boy and close cousin of Fr. Morgan, lost his two sons: the eldest in October 1914, and the youngest in April 1917. He was a prominent reminder of the conflict's victims.

---

2. When Galton died in 1928, he left some land and money for the construction of a church, Our Lady and St Hubert, in Oldbury, just west of Birmingham. The church was dedicated by the Archbishop of Birmingham on November 3th 1934 and the subsequent Mass was celebrated by Fr. Morgan, who had maintained regular contact with Hubert Galton, especially during his last years.

The Fulfilled Duty

The end of the war brought a change in Morgan's relationship with his wards, who were now adults, emancipated and with families of their own. However, this didn't mean the end of their connection, as suggested in Tolkien biographies which tend to omit any contact with Morgan after the war.

Hilary bought a fruit farm in Blackminster, east of Evesham, Worcestershire, and settled there. He had returned to where the Suffields, his mother's family, came from. Despite their religious differences, the Tolkien brothers still had a great bond with them. Thus, Hilary became an inhabitant of the beautiful Vale of Evesham, and there married Magdalen Matthews. The couple had three sons, Gabriel, Julian, and Paul, who were all born in the early thirties.

For the rest of his life, Hilary maintained a close relationship with his brother. Ronald and his family visited Blackminster regularly throughout the decades. They shared several important personal moments from Tolkien's life there; for example, when Ronald suffered a bout of pneumonia in 1923, he travelled there to recuperate; or the occasion of the maiden voyage of Tolkien's first car in 1932, where his whole family drove to Hilary's house.

Focusing on Ronald Tolkien's career after the war, it should be noted that he briefly returned to Oxford in late 1918 with his wife Edith and his son, John Francis. There, while working on the *Oxford English Dictionary* and teaching some classes (there was a lack of professors after the war), his second son, Michael Hilary, was born.

In early 1921, the family moved to Leeds, an industrial city in northern England, where Tolkien was appointed Reader in English. They remained there until 1925. It was one of the most professionally intense periods for him, as his academic career took off. He was made professor at the early age of thirty-two and his first works of significance were published, such as a new edition of *Sir Gawain and the Green Knight*, in collaboration with another scholar, Eric Valentine Gordon. The Leeds years didn't only revolve around academic matters though, as it was there that the family again grew, with the birth of a third child, Christopher.

When they arrived in Leeds, the Tolkiens resided briefly at 5 Holly Bank, in a house owned by an elderly niece of Cardinal Newman, which again suggests the mediation of Fr. Morgan, or at least of someone linked with the

Oratory. Afterwards, they moved to rental housing at 11 St Mark's Terrace, next to the University, and eventually bought their own home in the suburbs, at 2 Darnley Road.

To reach the centre of Leeds from Darnley Road, it was necessary to take the tram. Here we find a family anecdote involving Fr. Morgan. This event confirms how contact between the priest and his wards was maintained after their coming of age and allows us to discover a previously unknown fondness of Tolkien's. Priscilla Tolkien recounts the anecdote:

> He was a regular visitor to our family during the early 1920s when my parents lived in Leeds. This was some years before I was born. My mother told the story of going with Fr. Francis on the tram from the suburb where they lived into the city. Fr. Francis was anxious to buy a present and knew my father was particularly fond of camembert cheese, which was quite expensive in those days and so would be a special treat. It is a very strong smelling cheese and this one was extremely ripe, so my mother said the smell was quite dreadful, so bad that everybody else got off the tram and they rode all the way home having a whole tram to themselves.[1]

It seems that this innocent story remained long in the memory for the Tolkiens, retold over the years to the point where Priscilla, who hadn't yet been born when these events occurred, came to hear all about it. Roughly three years before her birth (in 1929, in Oxford), the family moved to Oxford, where Tolkien had been offered a post as professor, a professional success as well as the fulfilment of a longstanding wish.

Fr. Morgan's visits continued in Oxford. He was certainly a familiar figure, who awakes in Priscilla a vivid memory:

> I remember a very large man wearing a large cloak and, in spite of the authority and powerful presence that he conveyed, he was charming to me as a little girl.

This image is consistent with the descriptions of Humphrey Carpenter, Tolkien's authorised biographer, who wrote:

> Indeed, he was a very noisy man, loud and affectionate, embarrassing to small children at first but hugely lovable when they got to know him.[2]

His serious appearance often contradicted his unconventional personality. This can be illustrated unequivocally through two other family stories. The

---
1. This and the other anecdotes narrated in this chapter come directly from Priscilla Tolkien, and they have been transmitted to the author of this work through invaluable correspondence, because it gives a glimpse at some of the unknown Tolkien family legacy.
2. Humphrey Carpenter, *J.R.R Tolkien: A biography*, George Allen & Unwin, London, 1977, p. 34.

first brings us back to Leeds, in the early twenties, where the witness was Tolkien himself. He used to tell his children what happened one day when he got off the tram in the company of Fr. Francis. His daughter recounts it thusly:

> Fr. Francis was dressed in his cloak and was clearly an amazing sight for a local child, who stood and stared at him. Fr. Francis responded by sweeping off his large wide brimmed hat, bowing to her, and saying "Good afternoon" with great ceremony. After this, she ran away in terror!

In a sense, there is a certain parallel between the reaction of the girl and what happened to the troll in Tolkien's poem, *Perry-the-Winkle* (published in *The Adventures of Tom Bombadil*), who wanted to find friends among the hobbits, but his impressive appearance frightened them:

> He looked around, and who did he meet
> but old Mrs Bunce and all
> with umbrella and basket walking the street;
> and he smiled and stopped to call:
> "Good morning, ma'am! Good day to you!
> I hope I find you well?"
> But she dropped umbrella and basket too,
> and yelled a frightful yell.[3]

The next stanza continues the narrative and finishes with the verses:

> but old Mrs Bunce ran home like mad
> and hid beneath her bed.

These fragments are virtually identical to those in *The Bumpus* (although Mrs Bunce is called Mrs Thomas), the precursor poem to *Perry-the-Winkle*. It was written sometime around 1928 and was first published in 2014 in a new and revised edition of *The Adventures of Tom Bombadil*. *The Bumpus* is one of the *Tales and Songs of Bimble Bay*, a series of poems set in Bimble Bay, an imaginary English town situated on the coast. The dates are consistent, and this further reinforces the hypothesis, without any formal proof, of the possibility that the inspiration for trolls (or at least the troll poem) arose from this story of Fr. Morgan.

The second of these stories is extremely useful for understanding his multifaceted personality. It took place ten years later, over breakfast at 20 Northmoor Road (Oxford), the house where Tolkien wrote *The Hobbit* and *The Lord of the Rings*. The old priest was sitting at the head of the table and

---

3. J.R.R. Tolkien, *The Adventures of Tom Bombadil*, George Allen & Unwin, London, 1962, pp. 41-42.

Edith Tolkien asked him very respectfully what cereals he would like to eat for breakfast. Obviously, his position at the table and the respect respect shown to him by Edith were not accidental; he held these privileges as Tolkien's "second father".

Morgan chose a cereal called "Force", and he was helping himself from the packet when he discovered Priscilla, the youngest of the family, crying inconsolably. They were in fact tears of rage, because the priest had inadvertently chosen the girl's favourite cereal, and she regarded the packet as hers alone. Edith, her mother, was cross about this apparent rudeness; Morgan, realising the problem, stood up and bowed to Priscilla. Handing her the packet, he said: "Did I take the young lady's cereal? May I give it back to her and will she accept my apology?" By doing this, she was completely won over and her tears ceased.

His visits to Leeds and later to Oxford were not exceptional events and, on the contrary, they demonstrate his role as the elderly patriarch of the family. In fact, even on vacation, his presence was habitual. In 1928, he shared the summer holidays with the family in Lyme Regis, precisely where he had spent several summers with his wards when they were children. On this occasion, despite his old age, he showed his peculiar skills and John Tolkien, the eldest of Tolkien's sons, remembered many years later how the priest "produced a pile of marshmallows on top of an ant-hill, as if by magic".[4]

Fr. Morgan's death (which will be discussed in detail in the next chapter) was a truly sad event for the Tolkien brothers and their families. Priscilla Tolkien, as a firsthand witness of daily life at the Tolkien home, has a very clear memory of those times, despite being only six years old at the time. In addition to the cited anecdotes, she recalls:

> My other memory is of the time of his death and of the sadness I sensed in the house, and especially in my father, without my understanding at that time what this was about.

---

4. John and Priscilla Tolkien, *The Tolkien Family Album*, Houghton Mifflin, Boston, 1992, p. 61.

Last Years

The First World War caused a deep wound in British society. Arguably, the conflict was largely responsible for an overall change in ordinary life and, obviously, the Community of the Oratory was also affected. The priests who had been mobilised took a long time to come back, while some of them did not return until several years after the end of the conflict. The war brought a change in attitude for many of them.

After the war, the whole Community was disturbed by a proposal to move the school. This idea began with a group of alumni, and its acceptance signalled, according to many scholars, one of the most significant changes in the history of the Birmingham Oratory. Initially, the majority of the priests were against the move and even the provost, Fr. Richard Bellasis, opposed it because it implied that, in some ways, the Community would lose control and influence over the school.

The matter was highly controversial, but pressure from many old students prevailed and, thanks to Fr. Edward Pereira, who spent all his assets on the project, the new school headquarters opened in Caversham Park, Reading, in 1922.[1] Three priests from the Community moved to Reading, but the rest remained in Birmingham, with their tasks focused on religious issues.

Another ambitious project, of a personal nature, was carried out in the summer of 1922. Fr. Morgan and his brother Augusto, joining him from Spain, embarked on a long journey, with the final destination being Palestine, where their sister Isabel lived. She was a Reparatrice nun, under the name of Mary of the Blessed Realino. After crossing half of Europe, they finally reached Jerusalem, where they met Isabel, who was over sixty years old and deaf.

They also did some sightseeing and visited various landmarks. There they met Fr. Angelico Barsi, an Italian-American priest, who was the Prior of the Parish of Saint Philip Benizi of Chicago. This was the spiritual and cultural centre of the city's Sicilian neighbourhood. They were photographed with him, in front of the Dead Sea, on September 26th 1922.

Most likely as a direct result of her brothers' visit, Isabel moved to Spain. Her first destination was the convent of her order in Madrid but, in 1927, she moved again, to Jerez de la Frontera (near Port St Mary), where there was another Reparatrice convent.

---

[1]. Years later, in 1942, the school moved to its current headquarters in Woodcote, forty miles from London.

Isabel died before her brothers, and Augusto was granted leave to visit his sister on her deathbed. There, she commissioned him to donate money to the convent from her own legacy, since he managed the whole family's assets. When she died on May 10th 1931, the nuns gave him her personal crucifix, and Augusto kept it in his bedroom until his own death, at which point it was sent to Francis Morgan.

Augusto was wealthy; he had his own car (not many people owned one in Port St Mary) and he often used it to travel with his friends. His closest friend was "Almenas", whose full name was José María de Palacio y Abárzuza, Count of Las Almenas and Marquis del Llano de San Javier. They made several trips to, and shared many days at *El Canto del Pico*, the palace that Almenas had built in the early 1920s, near Madrid. Other friends included Fernando Van Zeller, a Portuguese vintner, Herbert Dagge, an English, pioneer of cycling in Portugal, Mrs Margarita Shaw, and his relative, James Morgan, who was his successor in the management of Morgan Brothers.

In his personal life, Augusto Morgan was devout, with an extensive collection of religious books which were always marked with his initials, AM. He never married, and therefore had no descendants (in fact, none of his brothers or sister did). However, during his final years, Augusto Morgan developed a close relationship with one of his nephews (to be specific, a second nephew) who would become his heir in Spain: Antonio Osborne Vázquez. Antonio would have a major role to play during the last part of Augusto's life, as he became an inseparable companion on tours and trips. After Augusto's death, he lamented the loss of his uncle in a letter to Fr. Morgan:

> You do not know how much I miss poor Augusto. I will go alone to all my future excursions. He taught me to travel.[2]

Antonio Osborne Vázquez[3] was born in 1903 and was the great-grandson of Thomas Osborne-Mann, and son of Tomás Osborne Guezala, who had run the family business since the late 19th century. The care afforded to Antonio by his parents was conditioned by the early death of their firstborn; he was called Tomás, following the family tradition. After that, his parents were extremely overprotective with their other children, particularly Antonio, who didn't even get to study in England and was always with them.

When he had just turned twenty, he finally obtained permission from them to spend some time in Birmingham. Fr. Morgan arranged his accommodation and joined him on several trips. He introduced him to the Cadburys, owners

---

2. Antonio Osborne's letter to Francis Morgan, January 10th 1933, Osborne Archive, (Translated by the author of this work).
3. He was the brother of Ignacio, José Luis and Juan, mentioned in previous chapters.

of the great chocolate factory, with whom Antonio established a good friendship (Morgan was already a friend of theirs), a close relationship that still exists even now between the two families. Likewise, the priest sought a particular English teacher, Miss Burd, who Antonio had fond memories of, mentioning her affectionately in several subsequent letters to his uncle.

When Augustus fell seriously ill, he was responsible for notifying any developments to his brother in England. There are several letters in Spanish from this time, between nephew and uncle, through which it is possible follow the advancement of Augusto Morgan's illness and his brother's anguish, separated by distance, awaiting the fateful outcome. Augusto died on the last day of 1932. His final moments were described by Antonio in a letter to Francis Morgan:

> Augusto did not lose consciousness until the last moment. Nevertheless, I dare assure you he did not suffer because, whenever I asked him how he felt, he replied that he felt no pain. He only said that he was very sleepy. While Fr. Gomez and everyone else were at his bedside, I can clearly remember how an hour before his death he said: "Father, Antonio, my brother, the other world." One of those present there, who did not understand, asked him, "Where? In London?" And Augusto quickly replied, "No, in Birmingham. He knows it." As you will understand, the translation of these faltering words is easy. He wanted me to inform you that he was very sick and, at the same time, he was saying goodbye to you.[4]

Issues related to the legacy of Augusto Morgan were particularly complex, because there were two wills, one in Spain and one in England. Augusto had retained his English nationality even when living in Spain, presumably to preserve the benefits of being a British subject.

His inheritance in Spain was not extravagant. Despite appearances, Augusto Morgan didn't own any large estates. It appears that the family houses had been acquired by his cousin Fernando Osborne, with Augusto being a usufruct while he was alive. His other possessions, all except for his clock, were given to his nephew Antonio, who had to inventory his goods in detail.

Quite the opposite happened in England. Fr. Morgan was repeatedly *inconvenienced* (in the words of his nephew) in taking care of the many formalities concerning the Augusto's apparently large English legacy. He had to pay many taxes; for example, in May 1933, he complained that he had already paid more than £2,000.

A particularly challenging matter was shipping Augusto's clock, an old family heirloom, to his brother in England. Back then, the ability to

---

4. Op. Cit. [2].

take assets or goods from Spain abroad was limited, due to the Republican government's measures to restrict this. As a result, the only way to move anything of value was to do so as if it were a personal possession. Francis Morgan wrote the following to Antonio in May 1933:

> I appreciate your interest in solving the matter of the clock and the chain. If somehow they could be brought to London, a friend of mine would bring them here. This could be done very easily since many of my friends, and friends of the Fathers, come here from London.[5]

In his answer, Antonio informed his uncle about his idea to travel to England and bring the clock himself, believing that he had almost persuaded his parents to let him do so. Unfortunately, he didn't get his wish. The family sent another nephew to England in his place, Rafael Osborne Guezala's son, Rafael Osborne Macpherson. Rafaelito, as he was known, brought Morgan the clock, along with Isabel's crucifix, which she had left behind after her death.

Rafael Osborne MacPherson went on to marry a rich Texan heiress named Claudia Heard, and became an important figure in the family. It should also be noted that he was a personal friend of the famous artist, Salvador Dalí, who he convinced to collaborate with him on some designs for the Osborne company. In addition, he was an innovator and promoter of new products for the firm. In the fifties, Rafael played a prominent role in the development of the advertising campaign for the famous Osborne Bull[6], which is now a symbol of Spanish culture. In this respect, he was as complicit as Antonio, and together they were able to convince Ignacio Osborne, the then chairman of the company, of the positives of this advertising idea.

His nephew's visit must have been one of Morgan's last pleasures. He still kept in contact with his wards, but his cheerfulness had largely decreased after the deaths of his two brothers and sister. Similarly, he drew scant comfort from the situation in Spain. After the fall of the monarchy in 1931, one piece of alarming news followed another, leading up to the subsequent outbreak of the Spanish Civil War. With his family living in Spain in a wealthy social position, and notoriously Catholic, the situation was worrying.

In addition to these social and political troubles, his precarious health

---

5. Francis Morgan's letter to Antonio Osborne, May 10th 1933, Osborne Archive, (Translated by the author of this work).
6. The famous Osborne Bull has become one of the icons of Spain. It is a fourteen metre long black silhouette of a bull, currently without a reference to any brand, which stands on hilltops and along the roadside throughout Spain. Originally, it was designed just for advertising the products of the Osborne company but, over time, it surpassed its origins and became a characteristic element of the Spanish landscape. Interestingly, Francis Morgan had a direct relationship with the main promoters of the Osborne Bull.

became a real issue. Not helped by his advanced age, his condition worsened, and he finally died in his room at the Oratory on June 11th 1935, at the age of 78. Fr. Philip Lynch, an Oratorian who had lived with him for several years, pointed out later in a beautiful epitaph how the Oratory was a duller place without him. At least his death spared him the stress of witnessing the terrible struggle between brothers which started in his homeland just one year later.

Tolkien was unable to attend the funeral of his guardian. However, his eldest son, John, who was also a priest and whose second name was Francis, was there on behalf of the family. Morgan didn't forget anyone in his will and, as evidence of the great fatherly love he had developed for the Tolkien brothers, he bequeathed to each of them £1,000, a handsome sum at that time.

In addition, the clock which had made its way to Morgan through such considerable efforts, was inherited by the eldest of his wards, Ronald Tolkien, who kept it in his studio throughout his life and was able on more than one occasion to get it repaired, despite its antique workmanship.[7]

Morgan's fortune was noteworthy, as he was the last member of his family and so inherited all of the family wealth. The remainder of his heritage, worth more than £25,000, went to the Provost of the Birmingham Oratory, as representative of the Community,[8] exactly as Morgan had stipulated in his will if all his siblings had died before him.

Francis Xavier "Curro" Morgan rests in peace in the cemetery for the fathers in Rednal, along with the other deceased members of the Community. These include Cardinal Newman and many others with whom he shared his life, from those distant days when, as a child, he arrived in Birmingham to begin his studies at the Oratory School.

---

7. The Tolkien family called it "the flip-flap" clock, because it told the time by flipping the figures over as though they were the pages of a book, and all the while making a slight humming noise. After Tolkien's death, the clock was inherited by his eldest son, John, who died in 2003. It's unknown what happened to the clock after that.

8. *Catholic Herald*, August 30th 1935, p. 19.

Epilogue

Intellectual Influence on Tolkien

Morgan's intellectual influence on Tolkien, beyond his religious instruction, has frequently been scorned. Even in that area, he has been considered as merely a guardian[1] and never described as a learned man. It has also been ignored that he completed higher studies in theology and had direct contact with one of the leading minds of his time, Cardinal Newman, as his assistant, friend, and one of his first pupils. However, it would not be too risky to say that Morgan's ideas in other areas, outside of religion, were also taken on board by Tolkien.

The author considered himself a conservative, but there was a contrast between his pacifist principles and his position on the dichotomy of "Progress versus Nature", as could be expected of a Tory born in the 19th century. There was possibly nothing that repelled him more than seeking justification for the spoliation of nature, and the destruction that this implied, under the flag of progress. As he saw it, such loss would lead to the disappearance of certain groups, such as the peasantry, which were, according to his ideas, the core of every civilisation.

Symptomatically, Morgan was from a conservative background. It is plausible to speculate that the notions expounded by three prominent figures in his family, namely his great-grandfathers Nicolás Böhl de Faber and Frasquita Larrea, and his great-aunt, Cecilia Böhl de Faber, were significant influences on him, from an ideological point of view.

His maternal great-grandparents were paladins of literary and philosophical movements with strong anti-liberal characteristics. Specifically, his great-grandfather, Juan Nicolás Böhl de Faber, was one of the main Spanish promoters of Historical Romanticism, a philosophical and cultural movement, which emerged as a reaction to the Rationalism and Classicism that preceded it. Any arguments about the merits of its principles immediately draw parallels with Tolkien's views.

Romanticism replaces reason as a system of ideas able to define the universe and the relationships within it by a combination of three components: sensitivity, imagination, and passion. However, Historical

---

1. The level of theological training received by Tolkien should not be minimised because of his deep faith (as a result of his personal circumstances and, in particular, the death of his mother). In this regard, he lamented the training his wife received during her conversion. "Edith was instructed in the Catholic faith by Father Murphy, the parish priest at Warwick, who did the job no more than adequately. Ronald was later to blame much on the poor teaching given her at this time." Humphrey Carpenter, *J.R.R Tolkien: A biography*, George Allen & Unwin, London, 1977, p. 68.

Romanticism, rather than being a literary movement, is a vital creed, with a committed activism that influences the behaviour of its followers. Passion prevails over reasoning as a guiding principle, so that romantic and religious feelings, and appreciation of nature, become defining guidelines to live by. Its followers also reject the social scene around them.

Specifically, in terms of the literary field, these principles give rise to an escape from reality geographically, with authors setting their stories in exotic places and, temporally, choosing periods such as the Middle Ages. On the other hand, nature is no longer considered a mechanical system and is instead defined as a living whole, in close harmony with man, sharing the same spirit.

Beyond this, the yearning to obtain infinite, everlasting, life is a decisive aspiration in those of a romantic character. While idealistic, the struggle to achieve it gives meaning to the finite. Complementing this, acting also as an impossible desire inherent to the intellectual form of Spanish Historical Romanticism (which was largely applicable to Juan Nicolás Böhl de Faber), is a craving for recovery of the past. The idea behind this is that a historical decadence exists at the zenith of Spain's most glorious periods.

In tune with this, the ideas of Morgan's great-grandmother, Frasquita Larrea, focused on the application of romantic concepts as a starting point towards an expressly popular form of Historical Romanticism. It involves delving deeper into the above principles, but inherently provides them with a foundation that could only arise from the Spanish context of the early 19th century. Thus, the concept of romanticism derived from this is more a system of feelings than one of thought. This is exemplified by the typically romantic reaction of the Spanish people to Napoleon's invasion of Spain, and their resistance to his powerful army using guerrilla tactics.

In several texts, Larrea exalted the War of Independence (which she witnessed) and linked several significant Spanish military victories, such as the Battle of Bailén, with the ghosts of deceased Spanish heroes, claiming that they had provided aid in combat. At the same time, her concept of the peasantry as holders of virtue, pillars of religion, and defenders of tradition, is also a topic reiterated by her daughter.

In the works of Morgan's great-aunt, the famous novelist Cecilia Böhl de Faber, there are vital, intellectual statements, which were certainly inspired by her parents, but also quite different in some ways. Traditionally, she has been considered the creator of the realist school, mainly due to her novels on mannerism and customs. However, this *costumbrism* is a characteristic that exceeds genres in its importance, because its ultimate goal was to state certain principles that Cecilia claimed.

It is hard to characterise her works superficially but, undeniably, the importance of tradition is indeed highlighted in them. Hence, one of her aspirations was the recovery of popular folklore. She persistently extols the rural world and, on the other hand, vigorously censures cities and progress; or rather, she argues for the importance of nature, as represented through peasants, and against industry, which was essentially a big monster for her.

> I have visited some of the great centres of modern industry, the main beacons of the supporters of indefinite progress for the future transformation of the world. [...] [The workers are] unhappy particles of a big monster that devours and transforms matter; a demanding, brutal, relentless and ruthless monster (since this is a factory today). They have no more rest than the sleep stipulated by the inexorable despot who benefits from that mine of blood and human life without any break beyond the roar of steam [...][2]

She is, in this context, the enemy of modernity, to the extent where she posits that it poses a threat to tradition and provides an excuse for the destruction of many intellectual and tangible values.

> How helpless I feel! Destroy and not rebuild; not even plant some trees. That culture uses nature, if it needs to, as a source of raw materials to carry out wasteful works! What charm the past has for poetic souls, and how the present time shows its prosaic spirit with its dismissive rancour towards it![3]

The similarities are remarkable, and many of the intellectual and essential foundations of Juan Nicolás Böhl de Faber, Frasquita Larrea, and Cecilia Böhl de Faber apply to Tolkien. It may be thought that this is just coincidental, a simple case of convergence, but the nexus represented by Morgan, and the correspondence of Tolkien's principles with those described above, as evidenced in his life and works, certainly give cause for reflection.

For example, the applicability of a romantic creed to Tolkien's personality seems clear, at least in his youth. He was able to fight for the survival of an "impossible" love, which met with opposition from his family (as represented by his guardian), society (given the problems caused by religious differences), and his own beloved (who even got engaged to another while they were separated).

Also, nature is a fundamental aspect in Tolkien's work. Although his childhood in the English countryside left a distinct impression on him, this was likely not the only reason that led to his continuous exaltation of nature. Throughout his life (and work) it was evident that he had an attachment to natural spaces, rivers, and especially trees and forests; their symbolism is

---

2. Fernán Caballero, *La Farisea*, Centro General de Administración, Madrid, 1865, p. XXXII. (Translated by the author of this work).
3. Fernán Caballero, *Cosa cumplida sólo en la otra vida: Diálogos entre la juventud y la edad madura*, Establecimiento Tipográfico de Mellado, 1862, pp. 181-182. (Translated by the author of this work).

widely repeated in his work: the Ents, the Trees of Valinor, *Leaf by Niggle*, etc.

Regarding the literary aspect, it is curious to see how the romantic concept of *decline and fall* is represented through Tolkien. A commonly accepted view suggests that Tolkien was inspired by a projection of Original Sin. However, followers of Spanish Historical Romanticism reflect on the existence of a zenith, located at a point in history (in their case, the so-called Spanish Golden Age), from which progressive degeneration begins. This seems closer to the truth than the idea of a fall from a heavenly beginning translated directly from a Christian religious concept.

This nostalgic spirit, which harks to a glorious and unrepeatable past, is recurrent in Tolkien's work. This is evident, for example, in *The Lord of the Rings*, when Elrond refers to the Last Alliance, during the Council of Imladris:

> Never again shall there be any such league of Elves and Men; for Men multiply and the Firstborn decrease, and the two kindreds are estranged. And ever since that day the race of Númenor has decayed, and the span of their years has lessened.[4]

But the defining feature of Tolkien's work is escapism. Much has been said about this; in fact, his essay, *On Fairy Stories*, largely deals with this subject. Tolkien's creation dovetails a spatially and temporary escapism in which we are transported to a strange world, familiar yet different; a *secondary world*, in his words, called Middle-earth. It is a place not belonging to our world (also known as the *primary world*), where we are located in a distinct period of its history (for example, in *The Lord of the Rings*, it is the Third Age).

Perhaps Tolkien even goes further than the Romantics, using this *secondary world* to project aspects of our own present age. Within it, he reveals longings and contemporary values, free from complex social burdens, and they are shown plainly and bluntly. But there is no eager moralising, or preconceived messages; he is merely telling a story: a *quest* story.

It is significant, however, that the protagonists of this quest are peasants: the hobbits, a modest people who base their existence on the traditions and enjoyment of simple things.

> [A people] more numerous formerly than they are today; for they love peace and quiet and good tilled earth: a well-ordered and well-farmed countryside was their favourite haunt. They do not and did not understand or like machines more complicated than a forge-bellows, a water-mill, or a hand-

---

4. J. R. R. Tolkien, *The Lord of the Rings. The Fellowship of the Ring*, Allen and Unwin, London, 1954, Book II, Chapter 2, p. 319.

loom, though they were skilful with tools.[5]

Tolkien wrote such descriptions with a flavour of *costumbrism*, typical of Cecilia Böhl de Faber. However, the subsequent adventures of the hobbits seems reminiscent of an epic vindication in line with her mother's postulations. In fact, the chapter "The Scouring of the Shire" from *The Lord of the Rings*, presents some interesting similarities with the behaviour of the Spanish people to the invasion of the powerful Napoleonic army. One of the highlights was a tribute to the fallen after the battle:

> At last all was over. Nearly seventy of the ruffians lay dead on the field, and a dozen were prisoners. Nineteen hobbits were killed, and some thirty were wounded. The dead ruffians were laden on wagons and hauled off to an old sand-pit nearby and there buried: in the Battle Pit, as it was afterwards called. The fallen hobbits were laid together in a grave on the hill-side, where later a great stone was set up with a garden about it.[6]

Similarly, one of the cornerstones of this chapter lies in the connection between good feelings and nature, in opposition to aggressive progress, which exemplified Tolkien's ideas in this regard:

> An avenue of trees had stood there. They were all gone. And looking with dismay up the road towards Bag End they saw a tall chimney of brick in the distance. It was pouring out black smoke into the evening air:
> […]
> It was one of the saddest hours in their lives. The great chimney rose up before them; and as they drew near the old village across the Water, through rows of new mean houses along each side of the road, they saw the new mill in all its frowning and dirty ugliness: a great brick building straddling the stream, which it fouled with a steaming and stinking outflow. All along the Bywater Road every tree had been felled.[7]

There are additional parallels, in *The Lord of the Rings* and other works, which should not be overlooked. For example, Cecilia Böhl de Faber published several collections of riddles (and also of proverbs and sayings) aimed primarily at children and youths.

One of the most shocking moments in *The Hobbit* is the riddle-battle between Gollum and Bilbo. Of course, solving riddles or puzzles to overcome challenges is been somewhat commonplace in heroic and medieval literature, and Tolkien explicitly expressed his debt to this type of writing as a source

---

5. Op. cit. [4], Prologue, p. 17.
6. J. R. R. Tolkien, *The Lord of the Rings. The Return of the King*, Allen and Unwin, London, 1955, Book VI, Chapter 8, p. 359.
7. Op. cit., Book VI, Chapter 8, p. 344.

of inspiration. However, since the adventures of Bilbo Baggins are directed at a younger audience, they are very much reminiscent of Cecilia Böhl de Faber, especially considering the complicity that is established with young readers.

In addition, some of the items she collected in the mid-nineteenth century coincide and have similarities with Tolkien's riddles in *The Hobbit*. In particular, one riddle she uses to describe the wind should be noted:

> Vuela sin alas,
> silba sin boca,
> azota sin manos,
> y tú ni lo ves ni lo tocas.[8]

Translated into English:

> Wingless it flies,
> mouthless whistles,
> handless lashes,
> and you neither see nor touch.[9]

Tolkien used the following in *The Hobbit*:

> Voiceless it cries,
> wingless flutters,
> toothless bites,
> mouthless mutters.[10]

Tolkien himself stated in one of his letters[11] how much investigation one should carry out for the sources and variants of the riddles in *The Hobbit*. Indeed, Douglas A. Anderson, editor of *The Annotated Hobbit*, undertook a task in this regard and was able to find the origin of eight of the nine riddles. For the wind riddle, he says:

> I can find no single comparable analogue to this riddle. However, traditional wind riddles often contain variations of phrase on the elements of "flying without wings" and "speaking without a mouth."[12]

---

8. Fernán Caballero, *Cuentos, adivinanzas y refranes populares*, Sáenz de Jubera, Hermanos, Madrid, 1921, p. 180.
9. Translated by the author of this work.
10. J.R.R. Tolkien, *The Hobbit*, Allen and Unwin, London, 1993, p. 79.
11. Humphrey Carpenter, (ed.), *The Letters of J.R.R. Tolkien*, Houghton Mifflin, Boston, 1981, Letter 25, p. 32.
12. J.R.R. Tolkien, *The Annotated Hobbit (annotated by Douglas A. Anderson). Revised and Expanded Edition*, Houghton Mifflin, Boston, 2002, p. 122.

To summarise, the ideological and literary coincidences, and similarities of these riddles, raises the possibility of some influence (albeit indirect and circumstantial) of Francis Morgan over Tolkien. This influence could mainly have arisen from the personal contact between them, through the oral transmission of traditions and ideas inherited from his family.

Tolkien and Cardinal Newman

J.R.R. Tolkien and Cardinal Newman share a number of important commonalities, both personally and intellectually. Newman was a leading figure of Catholic thought in his time, whose approach was, in many cases, entirely contemporary. Undoubtedly, he is a model for Roman Catholics (worldwide, not just in England) with his contributions to theological and doctrinal matters. Like other British Roman Catholic authors, Tolkien was indebted to the thought and ideas of Newman, but his case is unusual because he received this intellectual legacy firsthand, from Fr. Morgan.

John Henry Newman was born in London on February 21st 1801. He was the eldest son of a wealthy couple (his father was a banker), who were members of the Church of England, despite the Huguenot origins of his mother's family, who were from France. He was educated in Ealing, a private school where, at the age of fifteen, he discovered his religious vocation and decided to dedicate the rest of his life to spiritual matters. Later, he attended Trinity College at Oxford, and excelled in his studies, being ordained as an Anglican clergyman in 1825. He remained in Oxford and, within a few years, became vicar of the Oxford University Church of Saint Mary the Virgin, while he worked as a college tutor, and also wrote theological papers.

After his return from a trip to Italy, where he had been severely ill, he became one of the leaders of the so-called Oxford Movement, along with John Keble, Edward Bouverie Pusey, Hurrell Froude, and other Anglican clergymen. Initially, they departed from the principle that the Anglican faith was really a Catholic creed, though not subject to the dictates of the Pope. They claimed that its location on the map of Christian religions should lie equidistantly between Protestantism and Roman Catholicism, so this position was designated as *via media*.

Their desire for regeneration led them to fight against the evils that, according to them, threatened Anglicanism. This stance, viewed by many members of the Anglican church as revolutionary, led them to propose the reintroduction of Catholic principles such as devotion and tradition. This, however, caused the outright rejection of their ideas by the ecclesiastical authorities of the Church of England. The Movement, though, found remarkable acceptance within many clergies and the learned laity, and represented an important influence for them.

In the 1840s, Newman, together with a group of friends and disciples, went to a small town to the south of Oxford, called Littlemore. From 1845, he publicly stated that Anglicanism was more of an artificial, political creation than a religious doctrine derived from the teachings of Jesus Christ. He also declared that *the Truth* lay in the Roman Catholic Church and, shortly after this, he was received into her bosom. Two years later, he was ordained as a priest in Rome and returned to England eager to spread the Catholic message among his countrymen. He was especially keen to do so among the most privileged sectors (also the most cultured), as the Oxford Movement had caused a noticeable impact on them and there were a number of conversions.

Newman settled in Birmingham and founded the Oratory of Saint Philip Neri, just a few months before the "Papal aggression"; that is, the restoration of the Catholic hierarchy in England. Newman was a part of the controversies arising from this event and disarmed critics of Catholicism with works of great didactic and theological value, such as *Letter to the Duke of Norfolk*, and *Apologia Pro Vita Sua*.

At the same time, he felt a great inclination towards education, probably due to his work at Oxford (whose doors were closed to him after his conversion to Catholicism). Two of his greatest legacies in this area deserve to be highlighted. The first is his writings and ideas on education. These came to light when he went to Ireland soon after his conversion, to be the rector of the Catholic University. Despite the fact that the project failed, his reflections in *The Idea of a University* received enormous interest. The other, more fundamental legacy, was the foundation, management, and administration of the Birmingham Oratory School.

Newman grew old while the school developed and increased in prestige and the number of students it hosted. The school and the Oratory became his shelter during the last third of the 19th century, the final period of his life, the culmination being his appointment as cardinal in 1879. He died on August 11th 1890, and the epitaph on his grave, conceived by him, is probably the best description of his essence and convictions: *Ex umbris et imaginibus in Veritatem.*[1]

Just seventeen months after John Henry Newman's death in Birmingham, thousands of kilometres away in the southernmost part of Africa, John Ronald Reuel Tolkien was born. His father was a bank manager in Bloemfontein, the capital of the Orange Free State (a region of the now Republic of South Africa). Because of this, the man who years later would become a renowned professor and author, came into the world far from where he would spend his formative years.

---

1. "From shadows and images into truth."

Most of his childhood, which was marked by the death of his parents (firstly his father and subsequently his mother, who died shortly after her conversion to Catholicism), was spent in the Birmingham area. Before his mother passed away, Tolkien came into close contact with the Birmingham Oratory, a connection which increased after her death, when Fr. Francis Morgan became his guardian.

At that point in time, the figure of Newman was still very much alive at the Oratory, since almost all Oratorians had lived with him and developed personal ties. Nevertheless, it should be noted that few people could have had closer contact with John Henry Newman than Francis Morgan, firstly in his younger years as a student, and later as a member of the Oratory Community. Hence, it is difficult to imagine that, being a ward of Morgan, the author of *The Lord of the Rings* had no knowledge of the works and approaches of Newman.

Certainly, in the biographies of Newman and Tolkien, there is also a significant geographical coincidence, concerning the two cities with the most relevant role in their lives. The first is Birmingham, where Newman spent his more mature years (which includes most of his career after his conversion to Catholicism) and Tolkien spent his childhood and early youth.

From a sentimental and inspirational perspective, the most important city for them was Oxford. In the case of Newman, his years at Oxford represented the first of the two halves that diametrically separated his life. During this period, he was a student at Trinity College, then a tutor at Oriel College, and Vicar of the University Church. The brilliant erudition emanating from the ancient colleges filled his life and cultivated his intellectual aspirations. Had it not been for his religious evolution, Newman surely would had remained in Oxford his entire life, enjoying its cultural richness. In 1863, he wrote in his diary:

> O how forlorn and dreary has been my course since I have been a Catholic! Here has been the contrast - as a Protestant, I felt my religion dreary, but not my life - but, as a Catholic, my life dreary, not my religion.[2]

This duality is the inspiring element for the title of his novel *Loss and Gain*. In a format similar to Platonic dialogue, and certainly autobiographical, it describes the process of the conversion of an Oxfordian to Catholicism. Its protagonist, Charles Redding, who is his alter-ego, revives the steps Newman himself took during his conversion in the second third of the 19th century. Oxford's colleges, and the people who lived there (professors, tutors, students, etc.), are described in detail by someone who felt like a member of that world.

---

2. Ian Ker, *John Henry Newman. A biography*, Oxford University Press, Oxford, 2010, p. 520.

After his conversion, he had to leave Oxford, because the University was closed to Catholics. Moreover, the Catholic Church itself banned Catholics from attending traditional universities such as Oxford or Cambridge, as it believed them to be a danger to the young ones, who could be perverted by the Anglican majority. Newman discreetly and respectfully opposed indefinitely maintaining this prohibition, especially taking into account the changes in British society and the universities; he also believed that a good education was an important asset for a Catholic, helping to overcome many inherent problems of the religion. However, this rule wasn't revoked until 1895, five years after his death.

Tolkien arrived at the University in 1911, a lift over a decade after the lifting of the ban on Catholics from attending Oxford. For him, Oxford was also his particular promised land. There, he struck up friendships with people who shared many of the same ideas and aspirations as him, satisfying his thirst for knowledge. Times had changed, the Catholic situation had improved and, despite some signs of marginalisation, Tolkien was able to develop his life in Oxford, free of other concerns aside from his academic interests.

A century after Newman launched the Oxford Movement, Tolkien was one of the promoters of a club of intellectuals known as *The Inklings*. They were described, among others, by Walter Hooper, the personal secretary of C. S. Lewis,[3] as "the Other Oxford Movement". C.S. Lewis and Tolkien can be considered the leaders of this group, which was supplemented over time by figures like Charles Williams, Owen Barfield, Hugo Dyson, and other Oxfordian scholars, who were mostly Christians.

Like the first Oxford Movement, their position as a group was opposed to the fashionable cultural trends, because they supported naturalness and simplicity, as demonstrated in their own works, where the narrative played an important role. Then, the avant-garde movement reached its peak, and authors from the British Modernist trend became a point of reference. However, none of the identifying traits of these contemporary groups, such as the use of psychoanalytic techniques to describe the characters, as inspired by Marx or Nietzsche, the use of free verse in poetry (which often resulted in an artificial complexity) and, above all, an exaltation of agnosticism, can be found in their works, especially not in Tolkien's.

Thus, given the ideological and geographical coincidences, the words of Walter Hooper are pertinent:

---

3. Clive Staples Lewis (1898-1963) was a medievalist who developed his academic work at the universities of Oxford and Cambridge. However, he is probably best known for his facet as a polemicist on issues related to religion, following his conversion from agnosticism. His fiction too, aimed at young people and also adults, afforded him a remarkable celebrity status. On a personal level, Lewis was probably Tolkien's closest friend, with whom he shared literary tastes, opinions and philosophical approaches, although their relationship cooled in the last years of Lewis' life.

If Cardinal Newman had been alive at the time, this was the club in which he would have felt at home.[4]

---

4. Walter Hooper, "The Other Oxford Movement: Tolkien and the Inklings", p. 216, in Joseph Pearce (ed.), *Tolkien: A Celebration. Collected Writings on a Literary Legacy*, Ignatius Press, San Francisco, 2001. Walter Hooper was the personal secretary of C. S. Lewis and wrote a biography of him. His essay, "The Other Oxford Movement: Tolkien and the Inklings", which includes his own memories of the Inklings, was selected by Joseph Pearce for "Tolkien: A Celebration. Collected Writings on a Literary Legacy". Pearce himself contributes with an essay entitled "Tolkien and the Catholic Literary Revival", which addresses topics discussed in this chapter and focuses on the relationship between Tolkien and Newman, though he repeatedly falls into preconceived concepts and ideas. This is, moreover, the sin of many of the other essays in this book. For example, Charles A. Coulombe's vision of Fr. Morgan should be noted, from "The Lord of the Rings - A Catholic View": "described as a "Welsh-Spanish Tory", surely as Ultramontane a combination as one could wish for." This is simply an affirmation full of prejudice and ignorance of Morgan's historical and biographical background.

Tolkien and the Spanish Civil War[1]

When historical events are analysed in hindsight and evaluated according to contemporary parameters, rather than to the circumstances in which they developed, it is easy to reach the wrong conclusions – or, at least, to get a distorted view of the different attitudes of the participants and witnesses of those events.

An obvious example is J.R.R. Tolkien's stance on the Spanish Civil War, culminating in his discreet moral support for the "Nationalist" side, the insurgents led by General Francisco Franco, who toppled the Republican regime after three years of fratricidal struggle between 1936 and 1939.

A simplistic view of the matter could inspire a perverted syllogism: this support, combined with the character and nature of Franco's movement, implies that, in the political arena, Tolkien was a fascist. Such reasoning is baseless. Tolkien's position was not inspired by political motives nor by affinities with extreme right-wing ideas. Priscilla Tolkien, the author's daughter, commented that the "whole period of the Civil War cast a great shadow over my father's life and is a powerful and lasting memory from my childhood."[2]

Surely an essential aspect of these feelings was his emotional link with Spain, formed through his personal ties with his guardian, Fr. Francis Morgan. Priscilla Tolkien recalls her father "saying how terrible it would have been for Father Francis if he had been alive after the onset of the Spanish Civil War". Fr. Morgan died in 1935, thirteen months before the war broke out.

Morgan travelled to Spain almost every year, until he became too old to do so. His last remaining brother, Augusto, died in late 1932, after which nephews from the Osborne branch became his closest family in Spain, and he maintained a fluent correspondence with one of them, Antonio Osborne. In addition to discussing matters related to Augusto's legacy, Antonio kept him up to date with the increasingly turbulent events in Spain (many of the letters are preserved in the Osborne Archive).

After the proclamation of the Second Republic in April 1931, Spain hadn't been able to maintain any political stability: strikes, riots, and episodes of violence against the Catholic Church were frequent. On October

---

[1]. This chapter is based on the article "J.R.R. Tolkien and the Spanish civil war" published in the journal of the Tolkien Society, *Mallorn*, issue 51, Spring 2011.
[2]. From the author's correspondence with Priscilla Tolkien.

1st 1931, the newspaper *El Socialista* summarised the position of the left-wing parties: "The Roman Church... has added to our history the stigma of a tradition of bigotry, intransigence and barbarity, and must be destroyed."

A reflection on this situation is seen in a letter from Antonio Osborne, dated January 10th 1933, written not long after a spate of arson attacks on churches and convents all over the country.

> Now, more than ever, I would visit you, but things are not easy in poor Spain. The situation is getting worse! Thank God, we cannot complain as neither the burnings of temples nor the great revolutionary strikes have been noticed in Port St Mary.[3]

Morgan's reply shows that the worsening news from his homeland marked his last years with sadness.

> I think a lot of poor Spain: I pray for her daily, incessantly. I know the poor Queen came to London for a short time. You are quite right that the elections were very poorly conducted, as I read in a book called *The Fall of a Throne*.[4]

In brief, he mentions the visit of the exiled Spanish Queen, Victoria Eugenie, to London, and his opinions regarding *The Fall of a Throne*. His affinity with this book, written by Alvaro Alcalá Galiano, brings significant (indirect) information about his personal ideology and his intimate belief about how differently municipal elections (whose result caused the departure of King Alfonso XIII and the proclamation of the Republic) could have been managed.

Morgan was strongly affected by events in his home country and undoubtedly shared his thoughts with Tolkien – which might, at least in part, explain Tolkien's grief at the outbreak of the Civil War. Tolkien found few supporters of the nationalist cause in Oxford. Even his close friend C.S. Lewis (despite his indifference to political life)[5] was opposed to the uprising. In fact, Tolkien reproached him years later for his staunch opposition to Franco:

> C.S.L.'s reactions were odd. Nothing is a greater tribute to Red propaganda than the fact that he (who knows they are in all other subjects liars and

---

3. Antonio Osborne's letter to Francis Morgan, January 10th 1933, Osborne Archive. (Translated by the author of this work).
4. Francis Morgan's letter to Antonio Osborne, May 10th 1933, Osborne Archive. (Translated by the author of this work).
5. Related to the Spanish War, a student asked him for a donation to support the republican cause and Lewis told him that he never donated money "to anything that had a directly political implication". John G. West. "Politics from the Shadowlands: C.S. Lewis on Earthly Government". In *Policy Review* 68. 1994, pp. 68-70, p 68.

traducers) believes all that is said against Franco, and nothing that is said for him. Even Churchill's open speech in Parliament[6] left him unshaken.[7]

In Britain, support for the Republican side was widespread. It was a broadly shared (and maybe rather simplisticly) thought that the Republic represented the legal Government in a struggle against the obscurantism imposed by "traditional" Spain, as represented by landowners, the army, and the Catholic Church. But the Republican regime was overshadowed by the chaotic social situation in Spain, with a drift in its policies towards the extreme left and a meagre response to violence against these traditional interests, especially the Catholic Church.

Tolkien's support of the Franco movement rested precisely on his perception as a champion of the Catholic Church against communist menace. Hence, Tolkien's position was a consequence of his Catholicism. Indeed, Catholics thought the insurgents vindicated traditional values and were defenders of the Catholic Church against the dangers of communism and secularism – in Britain, only Catholics supported Franco's movement en masse.[8]

Catholic religious leaders approached the issue in a similar way. In Oxford, for example, the distinguished Jesuit, Martin D'Arcy, and Ronald Knox, Chaplain of Oxford University, publicly supported the Nationalists. However, the clearest evidence of the official position of the British Catholic Church come from the statements of the highest Catholic authority in Great Britain at that time, the Archbishop of Westminster, Arthur Hinsley.[9] In 1939, with the Spanish War about to end, he wrote in a letter to Franco:

> I look upon you as the great defender of the true Spain, the country of Catholic principles where Catholic social justice and charity will be applied for the common good under a firm peace-loving government.[10]

---

6. In May 24th 1944, Churchill gave a speech in the House of Commons supporting the Franco regime, showing his gratitude for its neutrality in the Second World War, which he considered a great service to the allies.
7. Humphrey Carpenter, (ed.), *The Letters of J.R.R. Tolkien*, Houghton Mifflin, Boston, 1981, Letter 83, p. 96.
8. Curiously, British fascist groups never were strong sympathisers for Franco's cause. Oswald Mosley, leader of the British Union of Fascists, stated arrogantly: "No British blood should be shed on behalf of Spain". Tom Buchanan, *Britain and the Spanish Civil War*, Cambridge University Press, Cambridge, 1997, p. 90.
9. Tolkien had an additional link with Archbishop Hinsley. Hinsley appointed David Mathew as Auxiliary Bishop. Mathew was the brother of Tolkien's good friend, Fr. Gervase Mathew, a Dominican scholar who lived in Oxford, working at Blackfriars College. Both Gervase and David had spent their childhoods in Lyme Regis. Here, Tolkien knew them from a visit with Fr. Morgan, who was a friend of the family, when they were all children.
10. Kester Aspden, *Fortress Church: The English Roman Catholic Bishops and Politics, 1903-63*.

The tone of this letter might easily give a false impression of its author, but we should not forget that Arthur Hinsley was dubbed the "hammer of dictators" in the Second World War because of his criticisms of fascist Italy and Nazi Germany. He was admired by Winston Churchill, who appreciated his ability to connect with British society during the most difficult moments of World War II.

These opinions reflected not only a philosophical issue about what principles should prevail in Spain, but also the painful reality of a bloody religious persecution. Neutral British historians, such as Hugh Thomas or Stanley Payne, pointed out this period as the historical era of greatest hatred against religion and described the persecution of the Catholic Church as the worst that ever happened in Europe.

British Catholics, who had been harassed for centuries, considered the attitude of their compatriots to be almost as outrageous as the attacks on the Church in Spain. Tolkien was quite explicit in this regard:

> But hatred of our church is after all the real only final foundation of the C of E – so deep laid that it remains even when all the superstructure seems removed (C.S.L. for instance reveres the Blessed Sacrament, and admires nuns!). Yet if a Lutheran is put in jail he is up in arms; but if Catholic priests are slaughtered – he disbelieves it (and I daresay really thinks they asked for it).[11]

The support of British Catholics for the "rebels" in Spain was hard for others to understand, given that it was too easy to link political alliance with Franco – and thus fascism – with religious concerns and the fear of communism. Catholics, however, were quite clear on the distinction. As Ewelyn Waugh (a Roman-Catholic) wrote: "If I were a Spaniard I should be fighting for General Franco [...] I am not a fascist nor shall I become one unless it were the only alternative to Marxism."[12]

However, support for Franco meant rejection from the intellectual community, as happened with Francis de Zulueta, *regius* professor of Law at All Souls College between 1919 and 1948, and Priscilla Tolkien's godfather. Zulueta was born in 1878, of Spanish and Irish ancestry. He was a naturalised British subject and lived in Oxford for most of his life. His father, Pedro de Zulueta, was the son of the second Earl of Torre-Díaz, also called Pedro, a Basque businessman who had settled in London. His mother was Laura Sheil, daughter of the late governor of Persia, Justin Sheil, and sister of Fr. Denis Sheil, a priest in the Birmingham Oratory, whom Tolkien knew.

Gracewing, Leominster, 2002, p. 99.
11. Op. cit [7], Letter 83, p. 96.
12. Joseph Pearce, *Unafraid of Virginia Woolf: The Friends and Enemies of Roy Campbell*, ISI Books, Wilmington, 2004, p. 257.

Pedro de Zulueta's only sister married Rafael Merry del Val, a nobleman and a diplomatic supporter of Alfonso XIII. They had four children; cousins, therefore, of Francis de Zulueta. The eldest son, Alfonso, was the Spanish ambassador to London between 1913 and 1931 (until the Second Republic was established in Spain). His brother Rafael chose an ecclesiastical career and became Cardinal Merry del Val, a Vatican official during the papacy of Pius X. The Cardinal died in 1930, but his brother Alfonso, and especially his eldest son, Pablo, were very involved in Franco's uprising.

At Oxford, meanwhile, Francis de Zulueta's standing suffered from his colleagues' general disapproval of his support for the Nationalists (and, after the war, his support for the Franco regime). The rumour spread that de Zulueta was a fascist aristocrat who considered his Oxford colleagues to be plebeians. The truth was rather different, as exemplified in the help he gave to several Jewish German professors who were persecuted by the Nazi regime, such as Fritz Schulz, and especially David Daube, who developed a deep friendship with Zulueta.

The rejection and disdain that Zulueta suffered was undoubtedly less than that of other intellectuals, such as the poet Roy Campbell, who Tolkien met in 1944, as described in a letter to his son Christopher.[13]

Specifically, Tolkien cites *The Flaming Terrapin*, published in 1924, which got Campbell immediate recognition in the British poetry scene, and *Flowering Rifle*, published in 1939, which instead received a very different reception among critics. Campbell's support for Franco was certainly detrimental to the response to this book and Campbell's image was seriously damaged.[14]

Campbell was born in 1901, in South Africa, where he lived before moving to the University of Oxford in 1919. There, he met people like T.S. Eliot, Aldus Huxley, Robert Graves and, after the success of *The Flaming Terrapin*, the Bloomsbury group, which was led by Virginia Wolf. However, after a painful dispute with them, he left England, moving first to France and later to Spain, where he arrived several months before the onset of the Civil War.

In the letter, Tolkien confuses some information about him, saying for example that he became Catholic when in Barcelona. Campbell did indeed live in Barcelona, but settled in Altea, a small town on the coast of Alicante. There, he was received into the Catholic Church. In mid-1935, he moved to Toledo and established a cordial relationship with the Carmelite monks of that town.

---

13. Op. cit. [7], Letter 83, p. 95.
14. C.S. Lewis was a merciless critic of Campbell (although Tolkien points to extra-literary arguments in order to justify the severity of his criticism, such as "there is a good deal of Ulster still left in C.S.L. if hidden from himself."), Op. cit. [7], Letter 83, p. 95.

When the civil war began, the monks secretly gave Campbell several manuscripts from St John of the Cross, which were being kept in the library of the convent, probably thinking that his status as a foreigner afforded him some immunity. Their fears for the safety of the manuscripts proved to be justified as, only a month later, all the Community members were killed and the library was burned.

The impact of these assassinations, in addition to his own ideas, led Campbell to support the cause of the insurgents and he tried to enlist in Franco's army. However, he never fought, or belonged to any armed unit, although he toured Spain during the war. Pablo Merry del Val[15] persuaded him to remain a civilian, because he was more valuable as a propagandist figure than as a combatant: the Nationalist cause needed "pens, not swords".[16]

His explicit support for the Franco movement aroused suspicion, and he was often labelled a fascist. In fact, Tolkien was compelled to explain the poet's loyalty, based on his later actions, arguing: "He is a patriotic man, and has fought for the B. Army since."[17]

Both Tolkien and Campbell had a declared animosity toward supporters of leftist ideas, and Tolkien's sketch of Campbell concludes by drawing a comparison with the Red intellectuals, which clearly reveals his dislike for communism: "How unlike the Left – the "corduroy panzers" who fled to America (Auden among them who, with his friends,[18] got R.C.'s works "banned" by the Birmingham T. Council!)."[19]

Tolkien's own political opinions were, however, more metaphysical than orthodox. Tolkien sought to explain them to his son Christopher in a letter written during the Second World War: "My political opinions lean more and more to Anarchy (philosophically understood, meaning abolition of control not whiskered men with bombs) – or to "unconstitutional" Monarchy. I would arrest anybody who uses the word State."[20]

His aversion to state control (and also the fact that communism was violently opposed to all religions, but particularly to the Catholic Church) led Tolkien to consider communism as a terrible and harmful approach; even during World War II he described the Soviet leader Josef Stalin, at the

---

15. Pablo Merry del Val, quoted above, was the son of Alfonso Merry del Val, cousin of Francis de Zulueta. In the Spanish War, he served as head of press for the insurgent government.
16. Op. cit. [12], p. 271.
17. Op. cit. [7], Letter 83, p. 96.
18. Tolkien refers to a group of poets that flourished in the context of Oxford University in the early thirties, known as the *Auden Generation*. This group of young poets, led by W.H. Auden and made up of Cecil Day Lewis, Stephen Spender, and Louis MacNiece, belonged to the first generation of British attracted to Marxism. Interestingly, despite their different attitude towards the Spanish War, and considering the fact that Tolkien criticised Auden's departure to America during the Second World War, they developed a cordial friendship several years later. Furthermore, their relationship debunks the myth of Tolkien's intolerance, because Auden was a leftist sympathiser and a declared homosexual.
19. Op. cit. [7], Letter 83, p. 96.
20. Op. cit. [7], Letter 52, p. 63.

time allied with Britain, as "a bloodthirsty old murderer."[21] Moreover, he declared "I am not a "socialist" in any sense – being averse to "planning" (as must be plain) most of all because the "planners", when they acquire power, become so bad."[22]

If not in the field of political theory, some could reductively argue that his imaginary world is connected with the "Nordic" basis of the Nazi model, because Tolkien recreates typical elements from north European traditional culture. Tolkien explicitly denied this and scorned the "Nazi Nordic nonsense" and its attitude "ruining, perverting, misapplying, and making for ever accursed, that noble northern spirit, a supreme contribution to Europe, which I have ever loved, and tried to present in its true light".[23]

However, critics of the second half of the 20th century censured Tolkien, either directly or indirectly, as did the socialist critic Fred Inglis, who wrote: "Tolkien is no Fascist, but that his great myth may be said, as Wagner's was, to prefigure the genuine ideals and nobilities of which Fascism is the dark negation."[24]

Regarding such arguments, we can only appeal to the many examples present in the cosmogony of Tolkien, contradicting similar criticisms, because the archetypes in Tolkien's works differ from these parameters.[25] At the same time, analysing them closely, we can also arrive at the opposite conclusion:

> Tolkien always denied that Mordor was intended as a representation of Nazi Germany, or Soviet Russia, but was quite aware of its "applicability" to the death camps and the gulags, to Fascism and Communism—as well as to other, more subtle or fragmentary manifestations of the same spirit.[26]

Perhaps a balanced view could most appropriately define the genuine "political Tolkien":

> So Tolkien himself can be classed as an anarchist, libertarian, and/or conservative [...] In a consistently pre-modern way, Tolkien was neither liberal nor socialist, nor even necessarily democrat; but *neither* is there even

---

21. Op. cit. [7],. Letter 53, p. 65.
22. Op. cit., Letter 181, p. 235.
23. Op. cit., Letter 45, p. 56.
24. Fred Inglis. "Gentility and powerlessness: Tolkien and the new class" in *This Far Land: J.R.R Tolkien*, Robert Giddings (ed.), Barnes and Noble, New York, 1983, pp. 24-45, p. 40.
25. Although several critics insist on a supposed apology of racial superiority in Tolkien (for example, because of his portraits of the Elves or the Mens of Númenor) there is an unquestionable sample closely linked to the background of this work: the civil war in Gondor, in which a desire for racial purity leads to despotism and destruction.
26. Stratford Caldecott, *Secret Fire: The Spiritual Vision of JRR Tolkien*, Darton, Longman & Todd, London, 2003, p. 2.

a whiff of "blood and soil" fascism.[27]

Thus anarchist, libertarian or conservative (but not fascist) Tolkien was undoubtedly a man committed to his ideas, particularly with the religious beliefs he had acquired in his childhood and, obviously, this background contributed to the establishment of Tolkien's own ideology.

Even more so, although Tolkien had strong individualistic ideas and opinions that were antithetical with totalitarianism, the religious persecution in Spain was crucial to his support of the Franco movement. Maybe, at first sight, his attitude after the outbreak of the Spanish War may produce disagreement but, in his historical and social context, it denotes coherence.

On the other hand, discussing a situation as complex as that in Spain during the 1930s pays no regard to current ideas of political correctness, and we have to take into account that it was not simply an issue of good versus evil. Privately, the Spanish civil war greatly affected Tolkien, and the way he behaved agreed with his own convictions. This should suffice.

---

27. Patrick Curry, *Defending Middle-Earth: Tolkien: Myth and Modernity,* Houghton Mifflin, New York, 2004, p. 38.

Barrels Out of Bond

It is common among people who have been seduced by Tolkien's books to try and locate the actual places which inspired the landscapes in his writing. It would be a real feat to compile a complete list of places specified as probable inspirations for Tolkien.

Britain holds the record for the number of possible locations. In some cases, there is a real basis, since Tolkien himself admitted certain influences, such as the Warwickshire countryside, as one of his inspirations for the Shire. However, many cities and shires fiercely compete (perhaps with pretensions more focused on tourism than on literary interpretation) for this accolade, claiming to be one of *the* inspirational places of Middle-earth. Located in the Birmingham area are the Two Towers (Edgbaston), the Old Mill of Hobbiton (Sarehole Mill), the Old Forest (Moseley Bog) and Rivendell (Rednal). In the Ribble Valley and the Forest of Bowland (between Lancashire and Yorkshire) are the Brandywine, Hobbiton and, again, the Old Forest. Brill, in Oxfordshire, is Bree. Devon and Dorset, in particular the city of Lyme Regis, represent the coasts of Middle-earth, etc.

Leaving aside the anecdotes, the historical and cultural context chosen by Tolkien for the development of his works, in particular *The Lord of the Rings* and *The Silmarillion*, apparently produces an environment whose sources arise from traditions and stories specific to the medieval culture of northwestern Europe. In fact, that passion for northern Europe, allegedly one of the foundations of his work, has been, to some extent, mythologised. However, Tolkien stated that northern Europe and its traditions didn't hold any special or sacred elements for him, as some critics have asserted. He added that any inspiration he draws from them doesn't necessarily imply any kind of exclusivity in his linguistic or cultural affections.

> The North-west of Europe has my affection [...] I love its atmosphere, and know more of its histories and languages than I do of other pans; but it is not "sacred", nor does it exhaust my affections. I have, for instance, a particular love for the Latin language, and among its descendants for Spanish.[1]

So, if northern cultures did not *exhaust his affections*, it isn't unreasonable to speculate on the possibility of stories he heard in his childhood about

---

1. Humphrey Carpenter, (ed.), *The Letters of J.R.R. Tolkien*, Houghton Mifflin, Boston, 1981, Letter 294, p. 376.

Spain, from Morgan, eventually also serving as creative stimuli for some scenarios and situations in his future literary creations. Additionally, the content of the many Spanish books in Morgan's library, which Tolkien used to borrow when he was a child, has never been taken into account as a possible source of inspiration.

Certainly, an important Tolkien character is based on Fr. Morgan; a character that is easy to recognise and is connected to one of his great stories: *The Tale of Beren and Lúthien*.[2] If Tolkien himself assumed the role of Beren, and associated his wife with Lúthien, who but Morgan could be the inspiration for Thingol, father of Lúthien, who assigned Beren an impossible task to fulfil as a condition for marrying her? Thingol did not approve of Beren, who was only a mortal man. Even though he promised his daughter that he wouldn't kill him, he sent Beren on a suicide mission in order to eliminate him without breaking his oath. Beren's task was to recover one of the *silmarilli* (gems of immense power) from the Iron Crown of Morgoth, the powerful enemy of all free peoples. After great adventures and obstacles, Beren, with the help of Lúthien, fulfils the mission, and manages to marry her. There is a clear parallel between the difficulty of the task set to Beren and Tolkien's feelings of helplessness when he was unable to continue his romance with Edith in 1910. Sometime later, there was a reconciliation, both with Morgan and with Thingol, and in both romances, fiction here mirroring reality.

Beyond this biographical parallelism, there are other connections which could have served as inspiration for Tolkien, and lead us to what he surely learned through his friendship with his guardian. In this regard, Tolkien's extraordinary knowledge of wineries[3] and river-transportation of wine and other goods must be highlighted. This is borne out in "Barrels out of Bond", from *The Hobbit*.

> But at one point where it passed under the caves the roof had been cut away and covered with great oaken trapdoors. These opened upwards into the king's cellars. There stood barrels, and barrels, and barrels; for the Wood-elves, and especially their king, were very fond of wine, though no vines grew in those parts. The wine, and other goods, were brought from far away, from their kinsfolk in the South, or from the vineyards of Men in distant

---

2. The Tale of Beren and Lúthien describes the adventures of the great lovers of Tolkien's legendarium. Beren was a mortal man and Lúthien was an Elven princess, daughter of the king Thingol and Melian the Maia. Beren and Lúthien fell in love and this love was stronger than the impossible quest set to Beren in order to allow their marriage, so that they finally achieved it. Tolkien shared his tombstone with his wife and he asked that the names of Beren and Lúthien were engraved there, what clearly attest that he identified their own romance with them.

3. Wine aroused great interest in Tolkien (though the origin of this inclination is not clear). During his time at Merton college, he was a member of the *College Wine Committee* and, for a time, Steward of Common Room, so that he held the master key to the college cellar.

lands.

Hiding behind one of the largest barrels Bilbo discovered the trapdoors and their use, and lurking there, listening to the talk of the kings servants, he learned how the wine and other goods came up the rivers, or over land, to the Long Lake. It seemed a town of Men still throve there, built out on bridges far into the water as a protection against enemies of all sorts, and especially against the dragon of the Mountain. From Lake-town the barrels were brought up the Forest River. Often they were just tied together like big rafts and poled or rowed up the stream; sometimes they were loaded on to flat boats.

When the barrels were empty the elves cast them through the trapdoors, opened the water-gate, and out the barrels floated on the stream, bobbing along, until they were carried by the current to a place far down the river where the bank jutted out, near to the very eastern edge of Mirkwood. There they were collected and tied together and floated to Lake-town, which stood close to the point where the Forest River flowed into the Long Lake.[4]

Interestingly, until the railroad between Jerez (in the interior part of the region) and Port St Mary (on the coast) was built, the main transport route between the two towns (especially from Jerez where the wine was produced in a greater quantity) was across the river Guadalete. Perhaps the reference in the text to wine from "kinsfolk in the South" is not entirely coincidental.

Apart from this, there are some curious similarities between the southern part of Middle-earth in the Third Age and the area of Cadiz (in southern Spain), where Morgan was born. First of all, the Mouths of Anduin and their navigability recalls two Andalusian rivers: Guadalquivir and Guadalete.

The Guadalquivir, the most important river in Andalusia (and one of the most important in Spain), is navigable all the way to Seville, the famous capital of the region. Linguistically, it has a striking commonality with the Anduin, especially considering Tolkien's interest in the etymologies and origins of words; both literally mean "Great River". Guadalquivir comes from the Arabic expression *Oued-el-Kabir* and Anduin is simply the conjunction of the words "river" and "great" in Sindarin Elvish. Moreover, these rivers are known colloquially as the "Great River", both in fictional Middle-earth and in Andalusia.

The Guadalete is also an important river in Andalusia. It flows into the Atlantic Ocean at Port St Mary, and the estuary has allowed ships to dock in the town since ancient times. This river originates within the province of Cadiz, and along its course there are places that were greatly valued by Morgan's family, especially the Osborne branch.

It was usual for the high society in Port St Mary to visit the small and picturesque villages away from the coast to enjoy their tranquility; hunting

---

4. J.R.R. Tolkien, *The Hobbit*, Allen and Unwin, London, 1993, pp. 170-171.

activities were also customary, as many of these places are surrounded by nature, set between hills and mountains, with some incredible landscapes.

Thus, going upstream along the Guadalete river, we come to one of its tributaries, the Majaceite, which threads its way through beautiful mountainous landscapes. It passes by places like Tempul, or the small town of Algar, where the famous *Pico*, or *Tajo del Águila* (literally "Peak of the Eagle"), is located; a triangular rock jutting from the hillsides above the river (today, a lake, after the building of the Guadalcacín Dam) with steps carved into it.

This rock is certainly reminiscent of the Carrock, a place near the house of Beorn, the man who could assume the form of a bear, where the eagles carried Thorin and company in *The Hobbit*. Incidentally, the name "Beorn", from the Old Norse *björn* (bear), is related to the surname Osborne, which is derived from, as Tolkien certainly knew, the Old Norse name *Asbjorn*: *ás* meaning "god" and, again, *björn* (bear). This, combined with the fact that Beorn was dressed, in early versions, in loose black fur down to his knees (just like the garb of the large priest, Morgan), certainly gives rise to reflection.

There are other attractive places surrounding Guadalete River. Near Algar, there is a beautiful mountain village called Arcos de la Frontera, one of the most impressive so-called White Towns, a series of villages that owe their name to their houses with whitewashed walls. Sitting atop an enormous stone promontory, which from some perspectives seems to cross the foundations of the city, Arcos de la Frontera, is a place where Fr. Morgan's relatives often went on vacation. The narrow and steep streets lead to the higher part of the town, where the tower of a castle still stands. As one climbs to the upper reaches, numerous arches (*arcos* in Spanish) indicate the different heights and levels.

Speculating wildly, is it possible that Arcos de la Frontera was the inspiration for Minas Tirith, and Andalusia for Gondor?

Appendix

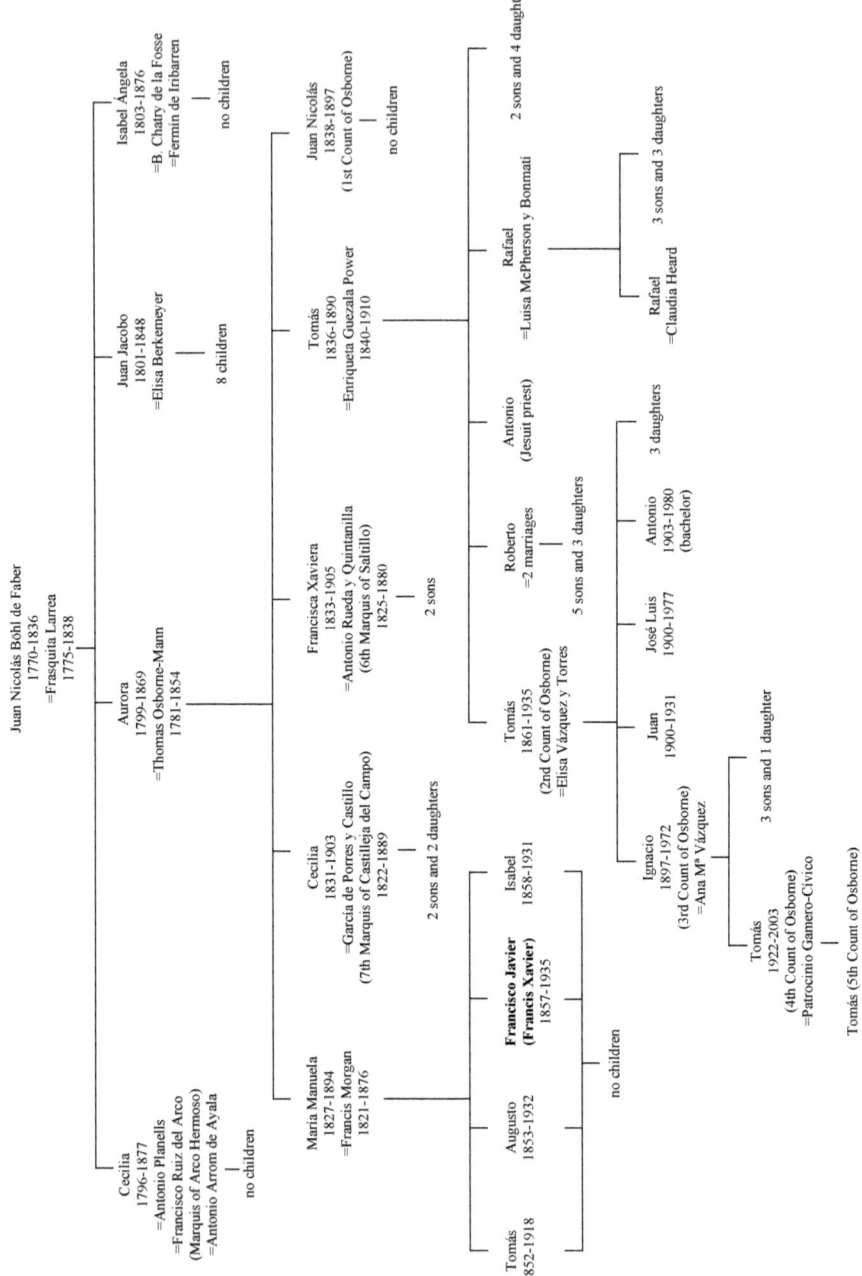

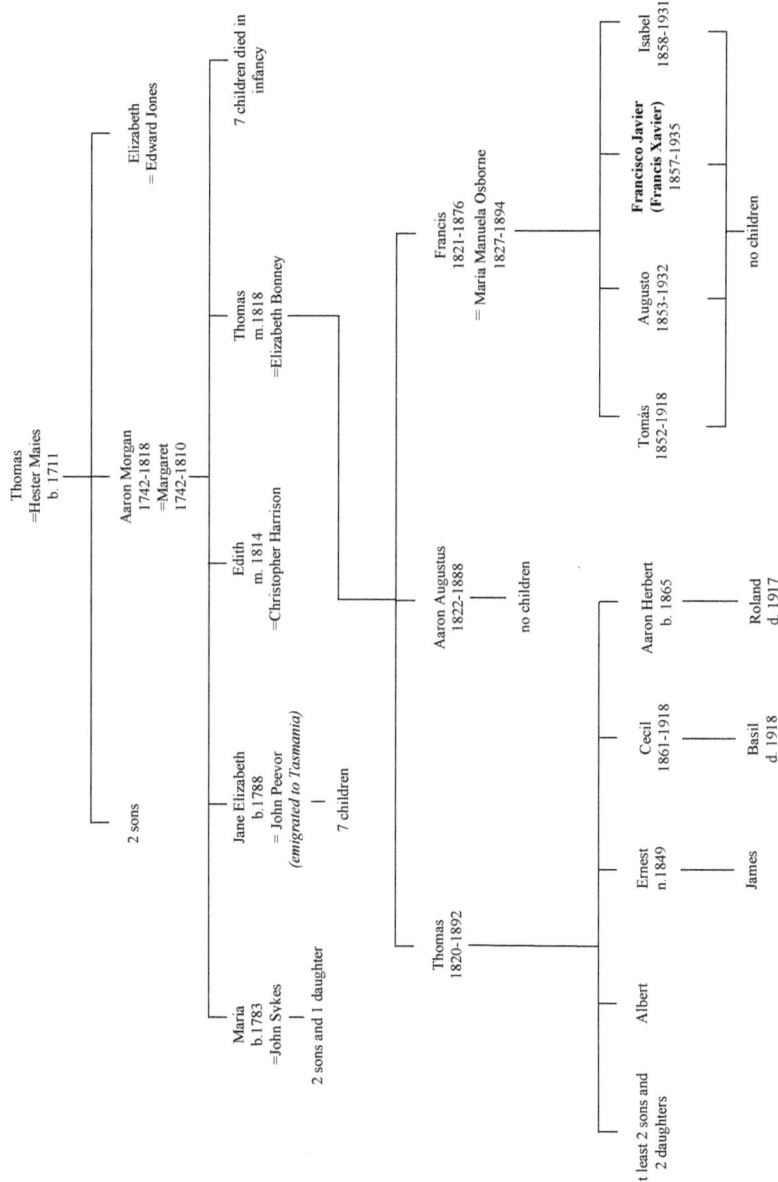

1

2   3

5

6

7

8

9

10

11   12

13

14

15   16

In affete Zio
Curro

Franciscus Morgan
et Osborne,
Cong: Orat: Pres:
apud Edgbaston.

Francis Morgan

1. Osborne Archive. Morgan-Osborne family. Circa 1865. Left to right. María Manuel Osborne, Francis, Isabel, Tomás, Francis Morgan, Augusto.

2. Osborne Archive. Francis Morgan. 3. Osborne Archive. Francis Morgan.

4. Birmingham Oratory. Standing (left to right): Francis Morgan, J. Norris, H.I.D. Ryder, W.P. Neville, G.L. Teeling, R.G. Bellasis, T.P.A. Eaglesim, H.L. Bellasis. Sitting: H.A. Mills, J.H. Newman, H. Bittleston, T.A. Pope.

5. Osborne Archive. Augusto Morgan and Francis Morgan. 6. Osborne Archive. Francis Morgan.

7. Osborne Archive. Francis Morgan.

8. Osborne Archive. With a boy. Lynton, August 1890.

9 Birmingham Oratory. Francis Morgan.

10. Osborne Archive. Francis Morgan and Augusto Morgan.

11. Osborne Archive. Fr. Angelico Barsi, Francis Morgan and Augusto Morgan. Dead Sea. September 26, 1922.

12 Birmingham Oratory. Francis Morgan.

13. Osborne Archive. Family House at Port St Mary

14. Osborne Archive. María Manuel Osborne Böhl de Faber (mother)

15. Osborne Archive. Francis Morgan (father)

16. Osborne Archive. Postcard (in Spanish) sent to Antonio Osborne. 1933

17. Osborne Archive. Signature as Tio Curro.

18. Courtesy Robert Hinii. Francis Morgan's exlibris.

19. Osborne Archive. Signature as Francis Morgan

Bibliography

Alonso, Sol y Lorente, Joaquín., *Osborne. Desde 1772 hasta nuestros días*. Bodegas Osborne, El Puerto de Santa María, 2005.

Aspden, Kester, *Fortress Church: The English Roman Catholic Bishops and Politics, 1903-63*. Gracewing, Leominster, 2002.

Baroja, Pío, *The Restlessness of Shanti Andia*. Signet, 1962

Bellasis, Edward, *"The Phormio" at the Oratory school, by an "old boy"*. Nichols and Sons, London,1881.

Bettonica, Luis, *El vino de Jerez*. Publicaciones Españolas, Madrid, 1974.

Buchanan, Tom, *Britain and the Spanish Civil War*. Cambridge University Press, Cambridge, 1997.

Buchanan, Tom, *The Impact of the Spanish Civil War on Britain: War, Loss and Memory*. Sussex Academic Press, Eastbourne, 2007.

Cadbury, Deborah, *The Dinosaur Hunters: A True Story of Scientific Rivalry and the Discovery of the Prehistoric World*. HarperCollins, London, 2001.

Caldecott, Stratford, *Secret Fire: The Spiritual Vision of J.R.R. Tolkien*. Darton, Longman & Todd, London, 2003.

Campe, Elisabeth, *Versuch einer Lebensskizze von Johan Nikolas Böhl von Faber. Nach seinen eigenen Briefen*. Als Handschrift gedruckt. Brockhaus, Leipzig, 1858.

Carmichael Calum, *Ideas and the Man: Remembering David Daube*. Vittorio Klostermann, Frankfurt am Main, 2004.

Carpenter, Humphrey, *J.R.R. Tolkien: A Biography*. George Allen and Unwin, London, 1977.

Carpenter, Humphrey, ed., *The Letters of J.R.R. Tolkien*. Houghton Mifflin, Boston, 1981.

Cayley, George John, *Las Alforjas, or the Bridle Roads of Spain*. Bradbury and Evans / Richard Bentley, London, 1853.

Coloma, Luis, *Recuerdos de Fernán Caballero*. El mensajero del Corazón de Jesús, Bilbao, 1928.

Curry, Patrick, *Defending Middle-Earth. Tolken: Myth and Modernity*. Floris Books, Edinburgh, 1997.

Dickens. Charles, *Nicholas Nickleby*. Penguin Classics, London, 1999.

Drout. Michael D.C., ed., *J.R.R. Tolkien Encyclopedia: Scholarship and Critical Assessment*. Taylor & Francis, New York, 2006

Dessain, Charles Stephen, ed., *The Letters and Diaries of John Henry Newman. Volumes XXVIII, XXIX and XXX*. Thomas Nelson and Sons Ltd, Edinburgh, 1961.

Fernández Poza, Milagros, *Frasquita Larrea y "Fernán Caballero" Mujer, revolución y romanticismo en España 1775-1870*. Biblioteca de Temas Portuenses, Ayto. El Puerto de Santa María, El Puerto de Santa María, 2001.

Fernández Poza, Milagros y García Pazos, Mercedes, eds., *Actas del Encuentro "Fernán Caballero, hoy"*. Biblioteca de Temas Portuenses, Ayto. El Puerto de Santa María, El Puerto de Santa María, 1996.

Garth, John, *Tolkien and the Great War: The Threshold of Middle-Earth*. Harper Collins, London, 2004.

Giddings, Robert, ed., *J.R.R. Tolkien: This Far Land*. Vision Press, London, 1983

Gladstone, William Ewart, *The Vatican Decrees in their bearing on Civil Allegiance: A Political Expostulation*. Harper & Brothers, London. 1875.

Gordon, José María, *The Chronicles of a Gay Gordon*. Cassell and Company, Limited, London. 1921.

Grotta, Daniel, *J.R.R. Tolkien: Architect of Middle-earth*. Running Press,

Philadelphia, 1976.

Harman, Thomas T. and Showell, Walter, *Showell's Dictionary of Birmingham. A History and Guide Arranged Alphabetically.* Cornish Brothers, New Street, Birmingham, 1884.

Heinerman, Theodor, *Cecilia Böhl de Faber y Juan Eugenio Hartzenbusch, una correspondencia inédita.* Espasa Calpe, Madrid, 1944.

Herrero, Javier, *Fernán Caballero. Un nuevo planteamiento.* Ed. Gredos, Madrid, 1963.

Howkins, Ben, *Rich, Rare and Red.* The International Wine & Food Society. Heinemann, London, 1982.

Jeffs, Julian, *Sherry.* Millers Publications, London, 2004.

Ker, Ian, *John Henry Newman. A biography.* Oxford University Press, Oxford, 2010.

López Argüello, Alberto, ed., *Epistolario de Fernán Caballero. Una colección de cartas inéditas.* Sucesores de Juan Gili, Editores, Barcelona, 1922.

Maldonado Rosso, Javier, *La formación del capitalismo en el marco de Jerez: De la vitivinicultura tradicional a la agroindustria vinatera moderna (siglos XVII y XIX).* Huerga y Fierro Editores, S.L, Madrid, 1999.

Meynell, Wilfrid, *Cardinal Newman.* Burns and Oates, London, 1907.

Montoto, Santiago, ed., *Cartas inéditas de Fernán Caballero.* S. Aguirre Torre, Madrid, 1961.

Morgan, Aaron y Matthew Concanen, *The history and antiquities of the parish of St Saviour's, Southwark.* J. Delahoy and J. Parsons, London,1795.

Neville, Rev. W.P., ed., *Adresses to Cardinal Newman with his replies, etc. 1879-81.* Longmans, Green, and co, London, 1905.

Odero. José Miguel, *Tolkien. Cuentos de Hadas.* Ediciones Universidad de Navarra, Pamplona, 1987.

Pearce, Joseph, ed., *Tolkien: A Celebration. Collected Writings on a Literary Legacy*. Ignatius Press, San Francisco, 2001.

Pearce, Joseph, *Unafraid of Virginia Woolf: The Friends and Enemies of Roy Campbell*. ISI Books, Wilmington, 2004.

Pérez Galdós, Benito, *Guerra de la independencia. Tomo II. (Episodios Nacionales)*. Algaba Ediciones, Madrid, 2008.

Priestman, Judith, *J.R.R. Tolkien: Life and Legend: An Exhibition to Commemorate the Centenary of the Birth of J.R.R. Tolkien (1892-1973)*. Bodleian Library, Oxford, 1992.

Scull, Christina, Hammond Wayne G., *The J.R.R. Tolkien Companion and Guide*. Houghton Mifflin, Boston, 2006.

Sellers, Charles, *Oporto Old and New: Being a Historical Record of the Port Wine Trade and Tribute to British Commercial Enterprise in the North of Portugal*. Herbert E. Harper, London, 1899.

Shakespeare, William, *Henry IV*. Simon & Schuster, New York, 2005.

Shrimpton, Paul, *A Catholic Eton?: Newman's Oratory School*. Gracewing, Leominster, 2005.

Story, Alfred Thomas, *The Life of John Linnell*. Richard Bentley and Son, London, 1892.

Tolkien, Hilary, Ángela Gardner, ed., *Black and White Ogre Country: The Lost Tales of Hilary Tolkien*. ADC Publications Ltd, Moreton-in-Marsh, 2009.

Tolkien, John and Priscilla, *The Tolkien Family Album*. Houghton Mifflin Company, Boston, 1992.

Valencina, Diego de., *Cartas de Fernán Caballero*. Librería de los Sucesores de Hernando, Madrid, 1919.

Vizetelly, Henry, *Facts about Sherry Gleaned in the Vineyards and Bodegas of the Jerez, Seville, Moguer, & Montilla Districts during the Autumn of 1875*. Ward, Lock and Tyler, Warwick House, London, 1876.

Ward, Wilfred, *Life of John Henry Cardinal Newman*. Longmans, Green, and Co, London, 1912.

Warner, Charles Dudley, *Washington Irving*. Nueva York, 1891.

Waugh, Evelyn, *Two Lives: Edmund Campion and Ronald Knox*. Continuum International Publishing Ltd, London, 2005.

Ybarra y Osborne, Eduardo. *Notas históricas-genealógicas y heráldicas de la casa Osborne, Guezala, Böhl de Faber y Power, con algunas alianzas que han contraído*. Sevilla, 1929.

Consulted works by J.R.R. Tolkien

Tolkien, J.R.R., *The Hobbit*. George Allen and Unwin, London, 1993.

Tolkien, J.R.R., *The Annotated Hobbit* (annotated by Douglas A. Anderson). Houghton Mifflin, Boston, 2002.

Tolkien, J.R.R., *The Lord of the Rings. The Fellowship of the Ring*. Allen and Unwin, London, 1954.

Tolkien, J.R.R., *The Lord of the Rings. The Two Towers*. Allen and Unwin, London, 1954.

Tolkien, J.R.R., *The Lord of the Rings. The Return of the King*. Allen and Unwin, London, 1955.

Tolkien, J.R.R., *The Silmarillion*. George Allen and Unwin, London, 1977.

Tolkien. J.R.R., Christina Scull and Wayne G. Hammond, eds., *The Adventures of Tom Bombadil and Other Verses from the Red Book*. HarperCollins, London, 2014.

Tolkien. J.R.R., *The Monsters and the Critics and Other Essays*. George Allen and Unwin, London, 1983.

Consulted works by John Henry Newman

Newman, John Henry, *Apologia Pro Vita Sua*. Longmans, Green, and Co., London, 1902.

Newman, John Henry. *Lectures on the Present Position of Catholics in England*. Longmans, Green, and Co., London, 1908

Newman, John Henry, *Loss and Gain. The Story of a Convert*. Longmans, Green, and Co., London, 1906.

Newman, John Henry, *Speech of His Eminence Cardinal Newman on the reception of the "Biglietto" at Cardinal Howard's palace in Rome on the 12th of May 1879*, Libreria Spithöver, Rome, 1879.

Newman, John Henry, *The Idea of a University*. Longmans, Green, and Co., London, 1907.

Consulted works by Cecilia Böhl de Faber

Caballero, Fernán, *Cosa cumplida sólo en la otra vida: Diálogos entre la juventud y la edad madura*. Establecimiento Tipográfico de Mellado, Madrid, 1862.

Caballero, Fernán, *Cuentos, adivinanzas y refranes populares*. Sáenz de Jubera, Hermanos, Madrid, 1921.

Caballero, Fernán, *La farisea*. Centro General de Administración, Madrid, 1865.

Caballero, Fernán, *The Sea-gull*. Richard Bentley, New Burlington Street, London, 1867.

Caballero, Fernán, *Un verano en Bornos*. Establecimiento Tipográfico de Mellado, Madrid, 1858.

Papers and articles

Bossert, A. R., ""Surely You Don't Disbelieve": Tolkien and Pius X: Anti-Modernism in Middle-earth.", *Mythlore* 25:1-2 (Autumm-Winter 2006), pp. 53-76.

Cunard, Nacy, ed., "Authors take sides on the Spanish War", *Left Review*. London, 1937

Espigado Tocino, Gloria, "Mujeres y ciudadanía. Del antiguo régimen a la revolución liberal.", *Actas del seminario: Mujeres y ciudadanía en el primer liberalismo español*. Universidad de Barcelona, Barcelona, 2003.

Hespelt, E.Herman, "Francisca de Larrea, a Spanish Feminist of the early Nineteenth Century", *Hispania* XIII, 3 (May 1930), pp. 173-186.

Lynch, Philip, "F. Francis Xavier Morgan", Chapter address on 16/11/1987 in Birmingham Oratory, http://www.birminghamoratory.org.uk/about-the-oratory/biographies-of-past-members/f-francis-xavier-morgan-1935/.

Rodríguez Caparrini, Bernardo, "Alumnos españoles en el internado jesuita de Beaumont (Old Windsor, Inglaterra) 1874-1880.", *Miscelánea Comillas: Revista de Ciencias Humanas y Sociales*, Vol. 70, N° 136, 2012, pp. 241-264

West, John G., "Politics from the Shadowlands: C. S. Lewis on Earthly Government.", *Policy Review* 68. 1994: pp. 68-70.

Tracey Gerard, "Tolkien and the Oratory", http://www.birminghamoratory.org.uk/about-the-oratory/tolkein-the-oratory/

Newspapers and journals

Birmingham Mail, Birmingham, 12/6/1935.

Birmingham Post, Birmingham, 12/6/1935.

Catholic Herald, London, 30/8/1935.

Evening Despatch, Birmingham, 12/6/1935.

Hobart Town gazette, and *Van Diemen's Land advertiser*, 17/3/1821 (National Library of Australia).

Hobart Town gazette, and *Van Diemen's Land advertiser*, 5/1/1822 (National Library of Australia).

Leamington Spa Courier, Warwickshire, Inglaterra, 3/10/1891, 14/4/1894, 20/2/1903.

Mallorn, The journal of the Tolkien Society, Issue 51, Spring 2011.

Oratory School Magazine, N°89, December 1935.

Parma Eldalamberon, No.11, Gilson, Christopher; Hostetter, Carl F.; Wynne, Patrick; Smith Arden R., 1995.

Parma Eldalamberon, No.12, Gilson, Christopher; Hostetter, Carl F.; Wynne, Patrick; Smith Arden R., 1998.

Revista Portuense (issues from 21/1/1894 to 30/12/1933), Archivo Municipal de El Puerto de Santa María.

The European magazine, and *London review*, Volume 31, 1797, Philological Society (Great Britain).

The London Gazette, 4/1/1907.

The Oratorian 2014, Oratory School, 2014

The Oratory Parish Magazine, May 1909, Birmingham Oratory. Reproduced in www.birminghamoratory.org.uk/about-theoratory/tolkein-the-oratory/

The Tablet, London, 15/5/1880, 26/3/1881, 11/8/1883, 21/1/1888, 10/3/1888, 19/7/1890, 30/12/1893, 8/6/1895, 23/7/1898, 29/10/1898, 15/4/1899, 3/8/1901, 21/6/1902, 2/8/1902, 2/4/1904, 6/8/1904, 29/10/1904, 2/6/1906, 13/10/1906, 7/12/1907, 6/3/1909, 28/10/1911, 10/4/1915, 22/4/1916, 2/10/1930, 29/10/1932, 4/3/1933, 15/6/1935, 22/6/1935, 31/8/1935.

Documents

Boletín oficial del Ministerio de Fomento, Volumen 26, 1858.

Bristol, List of Freeholders and Freemen, 1768.

British census 1841, 1851, 1861, 1871, 1881, 1891, 1901 and 1911.

Dixon, Morgan & Co, wine merchants, London: corresp. and accounts c1830-1950 (Mss 38311-15). Guildhall Library (London).

Libro de actas de la sucursal del Banco Matritense en El Puerto de Santa María (1921-1923).
(From the copy in the Archivo Municipal de El Puerto de Santa María).

Memorandum of the Association of Morgan Brothers (Wine Shippers) Limited. Waterloo and Sons limited, Printers. London 1898.

Memories of Maria Sykes. British Library, Asia, Pacific and Africa Collections. Private Papers [Mss Eur C799]. European Manuscripts in the Oriental and India Office Collections of the British Library.

Old Bailey Proceedings Online (www.oldbaileyonline.org), 26th October 1803, trial of Timothy Tool (t18031026-54).

Tasmanian Pioneer Index 1803-1899.

www.ingramcontent.com/pod-product-compliance
Lightning Source LLC
Chambersburg PA
CBHW042126100526
44587CB00026B/4188